The Yorkshire *Beer* Bible

A drinker's guide to the brewers, beers and pubs of God's own country

Simon Jenkins

GREAT NORTHERN

Great Northern Books Limited

PO Box 1380, Bradford, BD5 5FB

www.greatnorthernbooks.co.uk

ISBN: 978-1-912101-69-6

Design and layout: David Burrill

CIP Data

A catalogue for this book is available
from the British Library

Introduction

A little over 25 years since I wrote my first pub column for the Yorkshire Evening Post, the whole landscape for drinkers has shifted beyond recognition.

Though I played no part in it save for chronicling its progress, the growth of beer culture has given today's drinkers a host of taste experiences unimaginable just a few years ago. New brewers have come to the market, through sheer force of quality muscling in on territory once dominated by national brands. Where once the ale lover might have been happy to find a single Tetley handpump as a guarantor of quality, now they are beguiled by bewildering choice. Bars focussed on serving quality beer – whether on cask or keg, from the UK or further afield – have revitalised Britain's on-trade. Longer-established pubs have expanded their own repertoire to compete.

That there has proved to be a market for such variety has encouraged brewers to stretch out into styles which had once been forced to the margin – porters and stouts, fruit beers, milds and braggots – confident that there were drinkers out there, thirsty both for refreshment and enlightenment. India Pale Ale, once a niche product of a handful of brewers, has exploded into a global phenomenon, fuelled by dazzling citric hop varieties from the USA.

Even the humble Brown Ale has been given a much-needed makeover, while the stigma once attached to keg beers has been blown away by brewers demonstrating that crafted, quality beer can be dispensed this way. Similarly, cans have displaced bottles to become the packaging of choice for many new brewers targeting the off-trade, a move unthinkable even just ten years ago.

"When we got going there were about 500 breweries nationwide," says Robert Wiltshire of the Yorkshire Dales Brewing Company in Askrigg, one of many Yorkshire brewers who have been a part of this seismic change. "Now there are three times that many."

This book aims to demonstrate the county's sizeable contribution to this new world order. I set out with the intention of including every single brewery in Yorkshire. Though I found 178, it's clear that new breweries are opening all the time, so it's very likely that some – the newest certainly, but even some older, smaller brewers – might have slipped through the net. For that I apologise.

My book also suggests some of the great places where you can try these beers – some recommended pubs and a number of interesting crawls around the county's cities and larger towns. But these lists are not even intended to be comprehensive, so if your favourite perfect drinking spot missed out, please don't feel affronted, snubbed or overlooked. Yorkshire has just too many of them.

During my travels, I asked several brewers to offer a definition of craft beer. It's a question which has exercised many great minds over these last few years, and my most satisfactory answer came from renowned Yorkshire brewer Dave Sanders, over a pint at the Tapped brewhouse in Leeds: "It's a bit like jazz. It's hard to explain what it is and what it isn't, but when you hear it, you know it's jazz."

This book explores Yorkshire's remarkable contribution to this new jazz age.

Simon Jenkins, June 2017

Abbeydale Brewery

Unit 8, Aizlewood Road, Sheffield, S8 0YX; T: 0114 281 2712;
E: info@abbeydalebrewery.co.uk; W: abbeydalebrewery.co.uk

South of Sheffield city centre, well away from the brewing heartland of the S3 postcodes, Yorkshire's first brewery alphabetically namechecks Beauchief Abbey which thrived here until the ravages of the dissolution. Kirkstall Brewery is another which preserves an ancient monastic name. Beyond its regular range, which includes the amiably grapefruity **Deception** (4.1%), a former Sheffield Beer of the Year, Abbeydale produces an assortment of predominantly pale and golden specials. Their enthusiasm for experimentation is perhaps best illustrated by the strange, faintly antiseptic, gingery, spicy, **Orange Wheat Beer** (4.5%). Though not for the faint-hearted, the palate soon acclimatises to the left field attack of this cloudy, Belgian witbier.

🍺 Abbeydale Heathen (4.1%)

There is a moment, just as you prepare to take your first sip of this beer, just as your nose is filled with the wonderful heady zest of grapefruit and pineapple, that you wonder if you might have picked up a can of Lilt by mistake. The liquid is the same enticing gold, both have colourful cans – and that big fruit blast just as the beer crosses the threshold has all the sunshine zing of that totally tropical taste.

Yet as soon as it hits the palate, Heathen's hop character barges determinedly forward, throwing its big bitter weight about. And though there's a little spike of carbonation, there's nothing like the full-on fizz of a fruity pop. But in the aftertaste, more of the citrus emerges in a dusty dry finish.

Heathen is styled an American pale ale, and the significant hopping is very much a trademark of the genre, though this one's moderate strength and ultimately rather quaffable character ensure it remains right in the mainstream.

Acorn Brewery

Unit 3 Aldham Industrial Estate, Wombwell, Barnsley S73 8HA;
T: 01226 270734; E: info@acorn-brewery.co.uk;
W: www.acorn-brewery.co.uk

Dave and Judy Hughes used a redundant 10-barrel kit from a pub in the defunct Firkin chain to establish Acorn in 2003.

The brewery's one pub, the Old No 7 in the centre of Barnsley is a four-time CAMRA regional pub of the year. Rich and rounded chestnut-coloured **Barnsley Bitter** (3.8%) with its long bitter finish is perhaps their best-known product (see also p157). Others include ultra-pale session ale **Yorkshire Pride** (3.7%), a permanent bottled beer on P&O cruise ship Britannia, liquorice-accented **Old Moor Porter** (4.4%) and an **IPA** (5%) which uses a different single hop every time. A monthly-changing list of specials and seasonals complete the line-up; Barnsley beers are widely available in cask, keg and bottle.

🍺 Gorlovka (6%)

Strong dark meaty porters were exported from London to the Baltic states from the back end of the 18th century – and gained their Imperial title due to the enthusiastic patronage of Czarina Catherine the Great.

For a century a handful of the capital's brewers produced beers with this Royal name, but by the outbreak of the First World War this once lucrative trade route had all but dried up. The recent explosion in the craft brewing industry both in the UK and the US, has seen it come back into fashion.

Acorn's jet black, firmly bitter version is named in honour of the Eastern Ukrainian city twinned with Barnsley. It has a complex beefy taste that melds strong black coffee and dark chocolate and just a hint of coconut. Empirically good.

Ainsty Ales

Manor Farm, Acaster Malbis, YO23 2TY;
T: 01904 703233; W: www.ainstyales.co.uk

Ainsty Ales could well be the only brewhouse in Britain to have a piano in the corner, though the daily variations of humidity and temperature have forced it well out of tune. Named after the Wapentake of Ainsty, a medieval subdivision of the county, Ainsty finally put down roots in Acaster Malbis in 2016, having spent time cuckoo brewing with Brass Castle in Malton. Sharp and fruity **Angel** (3.7%) is their biggest-selling beer, though only their full-bodied traditional, English-hopped IPA **Kolkata Karma** (5%) strays beyond sessionable strength. Others in a curiously alliterative range include the gentle straw-coloured **Flummoxed Farmer** (4%) and the golden, more orange-juicey **Wankled Waggoner** (4.5%). "Wankled" is a dialect word for "unsteady", just in case you were wondering.

Stapylton Arms, Wass

All Hallows Brewery

Main Street, Goodmanham, East Yorkshire, YO43 3JA;
T: 01430 873849; W: www.goodmanhamarms.co.uk

The lively red-brick Goodmanham Arms is home and brewery tap for this 11-gallon operation, established by pub owners Vito and Abbie Loggozi. Their flagship ale is the dark and sweetish mild **Peg Fyfe** (3.6%) whose name honours a 17th century witch executed nearby. One of her victims was **Ragged Robyn** and there's sweet, biscuity, dark fruit notes and plenty of substance to the 4.7% deep maroon ale which takes his name. Golden **Wayward Angel** (4.2%) provides a palate-cleansing blast of sharp refreshing citrus.

The White Horse, Ampleforth

North York Moors pubs

The north of the county, whether east or west of the A1, has so many wonderful traditional pubs that it seems iniquitous to have to select just a handful to recommend. All these in the North York Moors are worth visiting, not least because they often stock beers from the breweries in this book, but so are very many more: The **Black Swan** at Oldstead, **Sun Inn** and **Black Swan**, Pickering, the **Moors Inn** at Appleton le Moors, **Stapylton Arms**, Wass, **The Inn** at Hawnby, the **White Horse**, Ampleforth, **Forresters Arms,** Kilburn, **George and Dragon** and **Lion Inn**, Kirkbymoorside and **Buck Inn,** Thornton le Dale.

Ampleforth Abbey Beer

Ampleforth, York, YO62 4EY; T: 01439 766811;
E: abbeydrinks@ampleforth.org.uk;
W: www.ampleforthabbeydrinks.org.uk

Fleeing France after the revolution, a community of Benedictine Monks founded Ampleforth Abbey in 1802, bringing with them the secret recipe for dark and full-bodied, spicy, biscuity Belgian Dubbel style **Ampleforth Abbey Beer** (7%). The monastic order continues to thrive, as does production of their single bottled beer, which has won a string of awards, including being named best drink in the 2012 Deliciously Yorkshire Award.

Atom Brewing

Unit 4, Food & Tech Park, Malmo Road, Hull, HU7 0YF;
T: 01482 820572; E: drinks@atombeers.com;
W: www.atombeers.com

"We didn't set it up to make beer," says Scotsman Allan Rice, rather knocking me sideways with the opening gambit of a conversation in his office above the brewery on the northern fringes of Hull. "Primarily we saw it as an educational outreach facility."

Allan has a degree in physiology, his wife Sarah a PhD in biochemistry, and it's their passion for science which drives Atom, an enthusiasm evident both in the names of their beers and in the regular educational sessions they lay on for students from nearby schools and colleges.

Allan recognises something of himself in the young people of Hull: "It's quite similar to my home town of Greenock. We want to inspire these kids to think that science can be relevant to them. Coming here they can actually use their mathematics, their chemistry, their thermodynamics, and begin to think: 'I can do this.'" He cites the example of one student who lacked confidence at college, but after sessions at Atom, where he was given the chance to trust his own knowledge and make decisions about specific gravity and fermentation times, he began to thrive in class.

Plans to move to a new site and quadruple brewing capacity will go hand in hand with plans to open a lecture theatre, laboratory and classroom. A further stage could be to establish a foundation, separate to the brewery, which would both support local charities and help young people to pursue their scientific ambitions.

Atom certainly do things a little differently – running beer schools for people to learn the process from start to finish, fronting up about brews which have gone wrong rather than pouring them quietly down a drain – and are in the process of setting up a 10-strong panel, who will be trained in the fine arts of tasting and take a key role in the brewery's future direction. "We're going to teach them how to tear a beer apart," says Allan.

Atom love the challenge of doing something difficult, a case in point being their full-bodied mini hop bomb **Schrodinger's Cat** (3.5%), which he admits is "a nightmare to produce" not least because it uses a novel mashing technique devised in conjunction with a Brazilian student. Characteristically, the very challenge of its brewing

Owner Allan Rice and brewer Jack Walker

secures this a place on Atom's core list, alongside session IPA
Quantum State (4.2%), **Pulsar** pilsner (4.4%) and the big-tasting
grapefruit and pineapple IPA **Phobus and Deimos** (7%) whose
spicy character derives from a big dose of rye in the brew.

"We want to be consistent, but we still want to experiment," says
Allan, explaining that of the 76 different brews tried so far, two thirds
have now been retired. Yet it is that restless spirit of adventure which
gives us the triple IPA **Mars** (11%), a quantity of which is being
matured in old Rioja casks; hop free beers **Isotope** (10%) brewed
with elderflower and bog myrtle and **Dark Alchemy** (4.9%) spiced
with coriander and cardamom; and the head-scratching **Crema** (4%)
which somehow manages to combine an aroma of sweet Skittles
and a taste of bitter coffee into a blonde ale.

There's no fining, no filtering: "We just do it all by time," says Allan.
"We do our analysis by sense."

In just three years, Atom has grown to become one of the major
success stories of the Yorkshire scene; a measure of that
phenomenal popularity is that when they bottled 12% imperial stout
Neutron Star last year, all 3,000 were sold in 15 minutes. By the end
of 2017 they hope to be exporting to 25 countries.

And in a year when Hull became a European City of Culture, the
three ale lines in the new art gallery bar have all been given over to
Atom beers. It's clearly a City of Science too.

BAD Co

Unit 3, North Hill Road, Dishforth Airfield, YO7 3DH; T: 01423 324 005;
E: cheers@wearebad.co; W: www.wearebad.co

Having honed his skills during numerous visits to many of America's great craft breweries, Paul Holden-Ridgway established a microbrewery for his customers at the excellent alehouse Blind Jack's in Knaresborough, before establishing BAD Co (it stands for Brewing and Distilling) in 2014.

Beers include the amber, big bodied **IPA Wild Gravity** (5.2%) whose slightly sulphurous aroma is soon displaced by some hoppy, oily, resinous character, zipped around the palate by some significant carbonation. On the brewery website, Paul recommends partnering this with Lebanese spiced lamb.

The pale ale **Comfortably Numb** (3.8%) with its significant mango notes is Paul's favourite from the range. "It punches well above its weight and is fantastic for summer barbecues," he says. And though the name is borrowed from Pink Floyd, he admits to something rather heavier on the stereo while enjoying a pint: "You can't go wrong with a bit of Black Sabbath with a Pale Ale," he says.

Other beers in the BAD Co range confirm a love for classic rock: **Love Over Gold** (4.1%) is a hearty blonde, **Satisfaction** (6.7%) a sturdy brown ale aged in bourbon casks, Hallowe'en special **Smashing Pumpkin** (5.5%) draws in autumnal toffee, spices and fresh pumpkin.

Heavyweight quantities of aromatic hops make their presence felt in the tropical fruit blast of **Whiter Shade of Pale** (3.2%) which is tempered on the palate by malt and oatmeal that drag the beer from the dangerous extremes of IPA into the drinkable pale ale mainstream.

🍺 Dazed and Confused (5.5%)

Just as kegs are now the vessel of choice for many craft brewers – even some who were once part of the real ale revival – so cans have become the favoured packaging for many looking to make big strides in the off-trade.

The Bad Co cans are of the type where the ringpull detaches the whole lid, converting your can into an aluminium tumbler, but I choose to decant this milk stout into a glass, releasing its pale, creamy head. And just sitting there, jet black and beautiful with its chocolatey, cappuccino aromas, it almost looks too good drink.

Almost, but not quite. The taste was never likely to quite match up to that visual promise, and yet it does pretty well, stroking the palate with silky waves of bitter dark chocolate, which recede into a strident smoky finish.

The blonde, busty, beer-bearing Britannia of the logo doesn't look like she would be bad company at all. "I wanted a woman, never bargained for you," as the song goes.

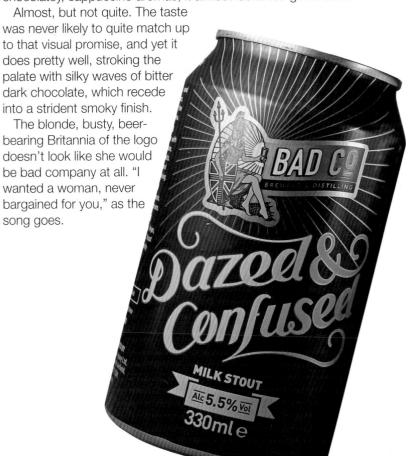

Bad Seed Brewery

7 Rye Close, York Road Business Park, Malton, YO17 6YD;
T: 01653 695783; E: info@badseedbrewery.com;
W: www.badseedbrewery.com

The natural haze which hangs in a Bad Seed beer
denotes a brewery which eschews fining and filtering to
derive the fullest aroma, flavour and body from its
bottled ales – most of which are vegan friendly.

Bad Seed was established on an industrial estate in
Malton by young actor Chris Waplington, whose CV
includes Pride and Prejudice, Much Ado About
Nothing, and Richard III – and who is now winning
ripples of appreciative applause for his beer.

The curtain rises with the slight, inoffensive **Aussie
Pale** (3.8%) and the story unfolds by way of the wheat,
spice, bubblegum and banana of **Hefeweizen** (5.1%)
and the surprisingly malty American Pale Ale **Cascade**
(5.4%) to the dramatic denouement of a silky, coffee-
ish dark ale that does everything you'd expect of a
beer called **Espresso Stout** (6.5%).

🍺 IPA (7.3%)

Brewed to a formidable 7.3% ABV, this cloudy amber
India Pale Ale is an absolute beast of a beer – and
perhaps requires a stage manager to step in front of
the safety curtain and warn that this is not a
production for the faint-hearted.

There's something of the passion fruit about the
aroma's opening salvo as you prise off the cap, but
this is immediately supplanted by big juicy, piney hop
resins which continue to dominate, right through the
taste, before just a suggestion of sweetness emerges
in the finish. If you love your bitter hops, love that
feeling of drinking something rich, substantial, almost
heavy, this could provide all the theatre you need.

🏠 The Maltings, Tanners Row, York

A commitment to quality cask and keg ale has made this quirky little warren an absolute legend on the local scene. Once you escape the busy traffic of Lendal Bridge and step inside, you are transported back to a simpler age when the perfect experience of enjoying a sociable drink and conversation wasn't diluted by the questionable fripperies of a juke box, fruit machine or television. Bad Seed is just one of many breweries whose products find their way into the Maltings' narrow, claustrophobic cellars. There can be as many as 40 different ones each month, with at least one mild and six ciders at all times. The display of mirrors and enamelled signs for products such as Hero Cycles, Royal Standard Lamp Oil and Black Cat Virginia Cigarettes wouldn't be out of place in the nearby Castle Museum. In a city well served by its pubs (see p37-38), this one remains my favourite.

Baildon Brewing

Unit D, Tong Park Business Centre, Baildon, BD17 7QD;
T: 07914 025148; E: leigh@baildonbrewing.co.uk;
W: www.baildonbrewing.co.uk

Biochemist Leigh Terry learned her trade at Shepherd Neame and after working in a cheese factory in France, returned home in 2014 to establish her own business. "The only thing I really know how to do is brew beer," she tells me over an afternoon coffee in the brewery on an industrial estate just north of Bradford. "So we sold the house and set up a brewery. Madness!"

And as a one-woman-band, Leigh not only has to brew the beer, she's also responsible for the sales, the deliveries, the paperwork and everything. Though a cancer diagnosis knocked her plans sideways, she is now in remission, and the business is back on track. "The brewery limped through for 18 months, and lots of new breweries came into the market during that time, but now we're ready to take the world by storm."

Her brewery is based in the former Denbirayne Dye mill – and it is perhaps that dyeing history which has led to her beer names being dominated by hair colours. There's a sunny, refreshing zestiness to the light and floral **Blonde** (3.6%): "You can almost get lager drinkers to try it," says Leigh. There's lots of nutty, maltiness to the robust, fruity and mellow ruby **Brunette** (3.9%); big and bold **Raven** (5.5%) is a fulsome, soporific plum porter; **Highlights** (4.5%) is an IPA specially brewed whenever there's an England rugby international, another of Leigh's passions.

Not all are hair colours. Golden, earthy **Sir Titus Salt** (4%) honours the local Victorian legend, and though originally brewed as a session ale for a Wetherspoon pub of the same name, its fame has spread to the point where it's now her biggest seller.

And Leigh's now planning for a 4% sessionable best bitter, provisionally named **Crowning Glory**. "A lot of brewers don't do a best bitter. They just want to do wild and wacky. But I think beer styles are good enough already, so I don't want to mess with them. Hopefully it can give Tetley and Theakston a run for their money."

Barearts Brewery

290-292 Rochdale Road, Todmorden; T: 01706 839305

The eye-catching pink Barearts Beer Shop and Gallery on
Rochdale Road in Todmorden is the only outlet for Barearts'
bottled beers which are brewed by Trevor and Kathy Cook. The
courtyard behind the shop opens out onto the Rochdale Canal
and the badlands of Lancashire are just a stone's throw west of
here.

Baytown Brewery

Fern Dene, Thorpe Lane, Fylingthorpe, Whitby, YO22 4TH;
T: 01947 880513; E: paul@baytownrhb.com;
W: www.baytownrhb.com

Search the Baytown website for the story of the brewery and you'll find a tall tale of contraband, hidden tunnels and secret recipes – and the ancient diary of a smuggler which revealed his scrapes with the customs men. Baytown was the 18th century locals' name for Robin Hood's Bay, and though the village's dramatic location amid the north Yorkshire cliffs may once have been the setting for this most ancient of criminal professions, the brewery's blurb of silly names and derring-do reduces it to a pantomimic Jamaica Inn.

Thankfully, there's some quality ale behind the hype. Pale and malty **Press Gang's Arrival** (3.8%) is their entry-level easy-drinking ale while the full-bodied **Smuggler's Haul** (6%) concentrates these flavours into a simple, bold, strong bitter. **Squire's Connivance** (5%) is a dark porter packed with chocolate, liquorice and aniseed, while the ruby ale **Whitby Heritage** (4.4%) features the work of famous local Victorian photographer Frank Meadow Sutcliffe on an eye-catching pump clip. Several of the Baytown beers are also available in bottle – and are served on the Newcastle-Amsterdam ferry too!

🍺 Baytown Bitter (4%)

The slightly sweet, butterscotchy ale pours an attractive pale golden brown, topped with an extravagant foaming head. While there's no significant aroma, once on the palate it charges around like a cutlass-wielding pirate, showing off its full-bodied malty weight. Only in the finish does the balance tip towards the bitterness of the hops, just as it should in a traditional, sessionable Yorkshire bitter.

A Whitby pub crawl

Like most seaside resorts, Whitby boasts more than its fair share of pubs – some favoured by the locals, others more squarely targeted at visitors. We start our circular trek at **The Station Inn** in New Quay Road a CAMRA favourite whose house ale Platform 3 comes from Whitby Brewery.

From here it's a short walk to Flowergate and the **Little Angel**, with its six real ales, before heading down to the quayside where the **Jolly Sailors** offers sturdy pub food and keenly-priced Sam Smith's booze. From here, cross the bridge and head into Church Street, where you'll find, reading north to south, **The Board** and **The Duke of York** close to the famous 199 steps to the Abbey, then the beautiful old **Black Horse** and the **Endeavour.**

But whatever you do, make room for just one last pint at the **Waiting Room**, a tiny but rather lovely new micropub in the station. Just along the coast in Robin Hood's Bay, the **Dolphin** offers the big name Masham ales. Five miles inland is the unspoiled **Birch Hall Inn** in Beck Hole.

Bear North Brewing

The Long House, Underbank Old Road, Holmfirth, HD9 1AS;
T: 01484 767954; E: info@bearnorthbrewing.co.uk;
W: www.bearnorthbrewing.co.uk

At 100-litres a brew, Bear North Brewing is as small as they come, producing seven ursine-themed bottle-conditioned ales such as nicely rounded traditional English bitter **Bruin** (4.3%), big-hopped juicy, citric American IPA **Grizzly** (6%) and tart raspberry saison **Arcadia** (5.2%). You'll find them at beer festivals and specialist beer stores.

Beespoke Brewery

The Fox, 41 Briggate, Shipley, BD17 7BP

The addition of a one-barrel brewing plant in the cellars brought a new dimension to The Fox, a popular modern freehouse just outside the centre of Shipley. Their standout ale is the sleepy, silky, delicate **Shipley Stout** (4.6%), while others include the gentle thirst-quencher **Plan Bee** (3.8%) and the firmer, darker **Beeboppalula** (4.2%).

Beak Brewery

12 Ryefield Way, Silsden, Keighley BD20 0EF;
T: 07985 708122;
W: www.beakbrewery.com;

Image: chloegrayson.com

Award-winning beer and food writer Daniel Tapper established his own brewery in 2014, developing innovative premium strength brews on his own pilot kit, before scaling them up using established brewers' plant.

He has four regular beers, including the straw yellow **Vermont IPA** (6%) which is named for the east coast state where Daniel sources the yeast which balances this assertive ale with some big peachy notes and no doubt contributes to this being among the least bitter India Pale Ales you're ever likely to find.

Juniper and pine-smoked lapsang souchong tea lend their influence to Daniel's smoky, resinous, berry-ish **Pinewood Smoked Pale** (6.2%) which is designed to be paired with smoked barbecue meats.

There are some appley, white wine and honey characteristics to the pale yellow **UK Sour Beer** (5.5%), brewed with 100% pilsner yeast and intended as a champagne-like beer to partner young cheeses.

A cocktail of seven malts, including several roasted varieties, engender the sublime coffee, cacao and tobacco flavours of **Export Porter** (7.2%) – and with its lingering briny finish it's a perfect foil for oysters.

Beer Ink

Plover Road Garage, Plover Road, Lindley, Huddersfield, HD3 3PJ;
T: 01484643368; ; E: Sales@beer-ink.co.uk;

The former garage site was first taken on as a brewery by Mallinsons in 2008, and also hosted the now-defunct Hand Drawn Monkey brewery, before Beer Ink began production there in 2016.

The draught beer range includes regulars **Avant Garde**, a bitter brewed with New World Hops (4%), **Pin-Up** pale ale (4%), **Noire** stout (5%), **Flagship** IPA (5%) and **Two Faced** Double IPA (7.5%).

Occasionals include **Mehndi** brown ale (5.2%), **One Armed Bandit** fruit sour (9.6%), **Hit the Road** pumpkin ale (5.2%), plus the red ale **Legion** (5.5%) which was brewed for the Royal British Legion and the Mayor of Kirklees. All are also available in bottle.

There is a small taproom on the brewery site, and Beer Ink regularly features in the Grove at Huddersfield, York's Maltings, Sheffield's Shakespeare and Fat Cat and across the Stew and Oyster Group. It has also made its way to pubs in Lancashire, Staffordshire, Lincolnshire and Shropshire: "Basically anywhere I can drive to and back in a day," says brewer Ryan Stoppard.

Bingley Brewery

2, Old Mill Yard, Shay Lane,
Wilsden, Bradford, BD15 0DR;
T: 01535 274285;
E: info@bingleybrewery.co.uk;
W: www.bingleybrewery.co.uk

Owner and brewer Darren Marks established Bingley Brewery in 2014 and has built a strong local reputation around an eclectic collection of products such as toffee and citrus blonde ale **Goldy Locks** (4%), roasted malt and liquorice stout **1848** (4.8%) and spicy, berry-bearing red ale **Blantyre** (5%).

Those for whom Bingley inevitably means the five-rise locks, should head for the sturdy, warming, deep brown **Lock Keeper** porter (5.7%), while drinkers who love their hop-front American-influenced pales will find the juicy, piney, slightly spicy **Jamestown** (5.4%) well worth a visit. Similarly, tart, golden **Tri-State** (4.5%) draws on the dazzling alchemy of Chinook, Centennial and Mosaic hops to deliver a draught of pinewoods, lemons and limes.

Bingley's bottle shop is open on weekdays; an on-site bar does a healthy weekend trade.

⌂ The Record Cafe, North Parade, Bradford

North Parade used to be the street for luxury goods in Bradford city centre; its shops were always a cut above. It seems it still is – the small fortune I spent on a triple-gatefold 12-inch record in pristine heavyweight vinyl at the Record Cafe seemed like money well spent.

When I chanced upon this place I was immediately taken by the concept of a bar where you can drink great beer, graze on interesting charcuterie food, and browse old-style record racks.

Keith Wildman's passion for music began as a teenager. "Weekends were spent going to record shops during the day and then going to gigs in the evening. When I first started buying records I had to save my pocket money, and then I'd get the bus into town, choose the record I wanted, have that whole ritual of looking at the sleeve, taking it home and finally dropping the needle onto it for the first time. It was an experience."

Even so, it took a trip to the 6-Music Festival for the idea for Record Cafe to finally crystallise: "There was a stall run by a shop called Pie and Vinyl in Portsmouth. They are literally a record shop that serves pies."

Back home in Bradford his idea took shape, with the concept based around quality produce, carefully curated. "I could tell you about everything here," says Keith, waving a hand over his four real ale handpulls, seven keg taps and towards the legs of cured ham hanging over the bar. "We opened in November 2014 and we're still here, so that tells you something."

The choice on draught changes all the time, and the current buoyant state of the craft beer market is such that few of them fail to sell to a knowledgeable clientele eager to try something different. The latest offerings are chalked up on a blackboard beside the bar. "We had an 8% Double Sour ale from Chorlton Brewery – and it flew out. And this is in Bradford, remember."

Black Sheep Brewery

Wellgarth, Crosshills, Masham,
HG4 4EN; T: 01765 689227;
E: reception@blacksheep.co.uk;
W: www.blacksheepbrewery.com

As a young man, Paul Theakston was heir to the Theakston empire, which had since its foundation passed to the eldest son. His father died tragically young, leaving Paul managing director at just 23. He brought in a cousin to help with the business – and though the arrangement survived 20 years, the loss of independence and change of lifestyle which came with the takeover by giant Scottish and Newcastle proved too much for Paul.

It's perhaps surprising the business didn't handcuff him from setting up in opposition. Even so, when he moved into Masham's old Lightfoot Brewery site, he found Theakston had registered the name, to prevent him reviving this well-known marque. This neat move forced Paul to re-think, and in doing so his wife Sue came up with Black Sheep, a name which neatly combines a reference to the town's sheep market, the maverick nature of the brewery's foundation – and a perfect marketing tool.

It would be a remarkable family that could survive such upheaval unscathed, and though the two sides of the Theakston clan come together to promote local events and tourism, the rifts have scarred but not healed. Both claim a unique bloodline to Robert Theakston, the first of the family to turn his back on their trade of cattle farming, when he took a lease on the town's Black Bull brewhouse in 1827. Theakston's have the name, Black Sheep prize their 'first son' provenance.

Townsfolk tend to take sides. Most have a connection to one or other brewery, and choose their pint accordingly. "Masham folk tend to drink either Theakston Best or Black Sheep Bitter," one local tells

Black Sheep head brewer Phil Douglas shows off Ram Tackle (4.1%) introduced in 2017 to celebrate the Six Nations Tournament and the Lions' tour to Australia and New Zealand.

me. The stronger beers – Old Peculier and Riggwelter – are "mostly for the tourists."

Of which there are plenty. Around 50,000 call in at the Black Sheep visitor centre every year, many joining the hour-long tour which winds through the site before ending at the attractive Bistro and Baaa'r (geddit), where a proud line of handpumps dispenses their stock products: dry, peppery, sessionable **Best Bitter** (3.8%), lemony, refreshing blonde ale **Golden Sheep** (3.9%), full bodied **Black Sheep Ale** (4.4%) and big-tasting fruit-cakey **Riggwelter** (5.9%). At first glance, the **Imperial Russian Stout** (8.5%) looks black as the ace of spades, but holding it to the light reveals its attractive deep red browns, while the aroma is red wine and smoky toffee. Caramel sweetness floods the palate and the tartness of blackcurrant develops in a long and significant aftertaste.

Each is brewed in traditional Yorkshire Square vessels – actually they are stainless steel and circular, but the process is precisely the same as when they were four-cornered and made of slate. A quarter of the output goes into bottles, the majority into casks.

Blue Bee Brewery

Unit 29-30, Hoyland Road Industrial Estate, Sheffield, S3 8AB;
T: 07375 659 349; E: sales@bluebeebrewery.co.uk;
W: bluebeebrewery.co.uk

Hefty, flag-waving quantities of mosaic, citra and equinox hops created the patriotic bugle blast of citrus and tropical fruit in Blue Bee's wonderful IPA **Born in the USA** (6%) which was Champion at Huddersfield Beer Festival in 2016. The brewery website lists this as a "past special", though they'd be well advised to bring it back to complement their light, summery, floral **Reet Pale** (4%), traditional bronze-coloured bitter **Hillfoot Best** (4%) and full-bodied but still easy-going coffee-ish **Tempest Stout** (4.8%). This ten-barrel brewery's relentlessly adventurous spirit spawns an ever-changing list of specials, seasonals, and occasionals.

🏅 The Kelham Island Tavern, Russell Street, Sheffield

If you only have the chance to visit one Sheffield pub, perhaps you should make it the Kelham Island Tavern. Despite the change all around this once industrial heartland, the Tavern has survived as a great purveyor of fabulous real ale. Bare floorboards lead to a simple chequerboard of tiles around an L-shaped bar topped with several banks of handpumps. On my visit, there was a real emphasis on Yorkshire, with beers from Abbeydale, Atom, Blue Bee, Bradfield and Brass Castle – and that's to say nothing of the other 24 letters of the alphabet. Regulars are greeted warmly at the bar; beer-tickers work their way through an ever-changing selection chalked up on the blackboard. Nearby, a museum tells the story of how Kelham Island once supplied steel and cutlery to the world.

Bob's Brewing – see Partners

Bobage Brewing

PO Box 96, Leeds, LS12 4XS; T: 07582 409682;
E: beer@bobagebrewing.co.uk; W: www.bobagebrewing.co.uk
Though apparently not closed altogether, all things Bobage seem to have gone rather quiet, which is a shame because this little Leeds outfit, with its Crew Brew and Wilsons Vintage names and the attractively amber, malty caramelly **No 1** (3.9%) was always worth seeking out.

Boothtown Brewery

4C Ladyship Business Park, Halifax, HX3 6TA; T: 01422 320100

The onsite brewery bar and bottle shop is the ideal place to make acquaintance with the products of a newcomer which has taken over where previous brewery Oates left off. Beers include the simple, red-brown session bitter **Proud Miner** (4%) and the sweetish, tropical fruity **Hoppy Valley** (4.5%).

A winning campaign

Now more than 45 years old, the Campaign for Real Ale (CAMRA) is one of the biggest and most successful consumer rights groups in the UK. The campaign was founded by four beer-loving friends in 1971 at a time when traditional handpulled British beer was being pushed out of the marketplace by giant brewing and pub conglomerates which saw greater profit in mass-produced keg ales. Their success is there for all to see, with new breweries opening all the time and drinkers being offered greater choice than ever. The remarkable resurgence in the popularity of beer has given brewers the confidence to revive genres of beer which were almost forgotten before CAMRA came along. And though keg beers were once despised by the campaign, the decision by many new brewers to concentrate production on craft keg ales has shown that characterful, flavour-rich beers can also be dispensed this way.

Bosuns Brewery

Unit C2, Wakefield Commercial Park, Bridge Road, Wakefield WF4 5NW;
T: 01924 671881; E: sales@bosunsbrewery.co.uk;
W: www.bosunsbrewery.co.uk

Grahame Andrews (senior and junior) share a
name and a military background – father in the
navy, son in the army. Brewing began in 2012
and though junior has now left the business, this
popular Wakefield brewery is going from
strength to strength, their beautifully-designed
naval-themed pump clips promise a safe haven
for any storm-tossed drinker. The no-nonsense
earthy, full-bodied brown ale **Maiden Voyage**
(3.9%) was the first Bosun's beer to be released,
and remains a local favourite. The softly sweet
tastes of lemon and peaches dominate golden
Bermuda Triangle (4.1%), there's some
substantial bitterness to **Golden Rivet** (3.7%) while **Pirate Mocha
Stout** (4.3%) and a good choice of seasonals freshen up the offer.

Bradfield Brewery

Watt House Farm, High Bradfield, Sheffield, S6 6LG;
T: 0114 285 1118; E: info@bradfieldbrewery.com;
W: www.bradfieldbrewery.com

Watt House was a working dairy farm before its diversification into
brewing; they went from milking 100 cows a week to brewing
100,000 pints of ale a week. The first pint was
served in 2005 at The Nags Head in Loxley which
is now the brewery tap. Smooth, floral and
copper-coloured **Farmer's Bitter** (3.9%) is their
entry-level product, with other permanent beers
including oat-enriched **Farmer's Stout** (4.5%),
dry and fruity **Farmer's Pale** (5%) and the big-
selling ultra-pale **Farmer's Blonde** (4%), while a
good list of seasonals completes the catalogue.
The brewery is a big sponsor of Sheffield's
phenomenally successful ice-hockey side the
Steelers.

Bradford Brewery

22 Rawson Road, Bradford, BD1 3SQ; T: 01274 397054;
E: hello@bradfordbrewery.com; W: bradfordbrewery.com

The arrival of Bradford Brewery in 2015 marked the end of a 60-year hiatus for brewing in the city centre. And a core beer range of a Yorkshire bitter, a pale ale, a brown ale and a lager suggests something refreshingly traditional about the values here.

Beers to look out for include well-balanced golden Yorkshire bitter **Northern Soul** (3.8%), Pacific-fruit influenced **Hockney Pale** (3.6%) and dry, smooth **Bradford Lager** (4.5%) which is dry hopped with Czech Saaz.

They've also diversified with seasonal specials including fabulous full-bodied, jet black, Turkish-coffee imperial stout **Lord of Misrule** (7.4%). Production is concentrated on cask, but the beers are occasionally bottled.

Odsal Top 4%

In today's bewildering beer world of imperial stouts, dark IPAs, sour gooseberry saisons, cloudy witbiers and unpasteurised lagers, the humble brown ale has become something of a forgotten style.

The time was when most British beers were a deep brown colour, before the advent of pale malt production in the 18th century gave brewers greater variety and greater reliability of production, largely reducing brown ale to some famous brands like Newcastle Brown, Sunderland's Double Maxim – and the softer, sweeter, milds which were particularly prevalent in the West Midlands. Each was the working man's drink of choice, relatively weak, keenly priced, and the ideal refreshment after a long day in the forges, factories and shipyards of industrial Britain.

Bradford Brewery has revived the style with this simple, well-balanced brown ale, named after a part of the city best known as the home of Bradford Bulls. Backgrounded by a blend of chocolate and biscuit malt, Odsal Top pours a deep red brown with soft malty aroma. On the palate, its initial tartness mellows with suggestions of toffee, biscuit and caramel before some red wine and woodsmoke arrives in a stimulating finish.

BRADFORD Brewery
ODSA TOP
A BRADFORD BROWN ALE

BRADFORD Brewery
ORD ISRUL
TURKISH COFFEE IMPERIAL STOUT

BRADFORD Brewery
OLERO
NGE & MANGO SUMMER PAL

Brass Castle Brewery

10A Yorkersgate, Malton, YO17 7AB; T: 01653 698683;
E: online@brasscastlebrewery.co.uk; W: www.brasscastle.co.uk

Though the brewery has long since relocated from Phil Saltonstall's one-barrel plant in his garage, Brass Castle Hill in Pocklington is now immortalised by his quality craft beers which have gained a following both in Yorkshire and overseas. Phil now divides his time between Malton and Boston, Massachusetts, while the brewery, based in slightly ramshackle premises behind Malton's main shopping street, is going from strength to strength.

Upstairs, between racks of pumpclips, brewing kit and promotional T-shirts, Sales and Accounts Manager Benjamin Voke talks me through the range. **Session Mini** (3.5%) is a hop bomb low in ABV but high in flavour, rye malt lends a spicy, earthy richness to **Tail Gunner** (4%) and three US hop varieties provide the juicy, fruity backbone to frontline IPA **Sunshine** (5.7%). American pale ale **Misfit** (4.3%) uses different hop varieties with every brew, the taste combinations varying with each recipe.

Vanilla porter **Bad Kitty** (5.5%) was the second beer Phil ever brewed, picked up first prize at York Beer Festival, and remains very popular. "To some people we are still the Bad Kitty brewery," says Benjamin. Even so, it is the **Helles** (4.4%), based on the light Munich lager style, which remains the brewery's biggest seller.

Currently open just from Thursday to Sunday, a rather singular taproom brings an extra dimension to the business. Drinkers lounge on upholstered hop sacks, the floorboards were salvaged from an old hospital, the curved staves of a beer barrel have been re-purposed as a chunky oak mural. "Our first bar was made out of an old wardrobe," says Benjamin. The taproom brings something different to a town whose licensed scene is fiercely traditional: "We're getting a lot of people coming in, so we're obviously filling a hole in the local market."

🍺 **Hoptical Illusion** (4.3%)

All the Brass Castle beers are vegan and vegetarian friendly – but this one is also gluten-free. Animal-derived products aren't allowed near the brewhouse, and a commitment to ecology extends to spent hops enriching the produce of local allotments and spent grain being used to create biogas and fertiliser. Hoptical Illusion is the gluten-free version of their single hopped Comet pale ale. It pours a dull, slightly cloudy pale gold, and has a beautiful rich, dry, bitterness to the taste, no doubt the product of the hops, but not overly citric, fruity or piney – and with absolutely bags of taste for a beer of its moderate strength. It even delivers a little warming glow in the finish.

Brew York

Unit 6, Enterprise Complex, Walmgate, York, YO1 9TT;
T: 01904 848448; E: info@brewyork.co.uk; W: www.brewyork.co.uk

Brew York burst spectacularly onto the local scene in 2016, shrugging off the significant setback of metre-deep flooding to their riverside premises just three weeks after signing the lease. The on-site taproom and stunning beer garden look out over the water. With its luscious, lustrous, sweet black darkness, the coconut, tonka bean, vanilla and cacao milk stout **Tonkoko** (4.3%) earned the brewery some early fame, with first prize at the city's beer festival. Other brews include the smoky porter **Viking DNA** (5%), session **IPA Little Eagle** (4.5%) and malty bitter **Maris The Otter** (3.9%). With its bold tropical fruit flavours, the American pale ale **Brew York Brew York** (4.9%) is so good they named it twice; the bags of sweet clementine to emerge from golden **Jarsa** (3.7%) belie its sessionable strength. New equipment has pushed capacity to 70 barrels, flood protection measures guard against a future swelling of the Foss.

A York pub crawl

A gorgeous miscellany of pubs thrives in the scrawling ancient grid of York. This circular route from the railway station offers something for the hard-core beer enthusiasts and those just as interested in the pubs themselves.

After a swift one at the beautifully restored **York Tap** on the platform, head across the traffic to the **Maltings** (see p 15). From here, continue uphill towards the Minster before turning left into High Petergate to reach York Brewery's **Three Legged Mare**, whose name honours the local gallows. Pass back across the west door of the Minster and into Stonegate and the fabulous **House of the Trembling Madness** which has surely the biggest beer selection in the city – with an eclectic choice both in the bottle shop downstairs and on the bar in the characterful, timber-framed attic. Around the corner in Little Stonegate, the basement bar **Sotano** may not be cheap but showcases superb keg beers from breweries rarely seen in York.

Progressing steadily south east, we reach **Pivni** in Patrick Pool, a cosy craft ale treasure house which seems utterly fitted to its timber-framed 16th century home. **The Last Drop Inn** in Colliergate is

House of the Trembling Madness

another York Brewery alehouse whose name recalls the city's taste for capital punishment.

Heading down Fossgate we reach the **Blue Bell**, York's smallest and best-preserved historic pub; across the road, but worlds apart, is **The Hop** where live music and tremendous pizzas provide a counterpoint to the quality Ossett Brewery ales.

Cross the Foss to reach the **Walmgate Alehouse** and **Brew York**'s riverside tap, before winding north and west to Sam Smith's famous **King's Arms**, always the first to fall victim to the Ouse's frequent floods. Crossing the bridge in Micklegate we reach the **Falcon Tap** and then **Brigantes**, part of the well-managed Market Town Taverns chain. From here it's a short stagger back to the station.

This is not a comprehensive list. Those of still greater stamina might detour to the **Royal Oak** in Goodramgate, or south of the city centre to the beautiful old cask-focussed **Swan** in Bishopgate Street with its Treboom-brewed house ale, and the nearby community-owned **Golden Ball** in Victor Street. Either side of the south-eastern Roman wall are the **Phoenix** in George Street and the **Rook and Gaskill** in Lawrence Street, CAMRA's 2016 York pub of the year.

Bricknell Brewery

Hull;
E: richard@bricknellbrewery.co.uk;
W: www.bricknellbrewery.co.uk

Tiny Bricknell is the very essence of a one-man band. It was established by former Hull University lecturer Richard English in his garage in 2015 – and he does everything from the brewing, bottling, label sticking and delivery himself. With a typical brew size of just 160 litres, Richard specialises in the production of unusual hand-crafted bottle-conditioned beers for local bars and restaurants. "I'm selling everything I produce, so I must be doing something right," he says.

His range starts with straw-coloured **Saazy Blonde** (4.2%) a crisp and fresh tasting real ale targeted at the lager drinkers. **Cascade Pale** (4.6%) is an American-style pale ale, brewed with lashings of Cascade hops which exert an energetic grapefruit influence on the aroma and flavour.

His stronger ales include malty, slightly sweet, dark ruby ale **Bosphorous 1875** (6%), based on a Victorian recipe, and Imperial Russian Stout **Slavanka 1873** (7%), named after a ship built in Hull for the Russian Tsars. For those who like drinking at the extremes, Richard's Belgian-style **Meaux Abbey Ale** (9%) uses pale malts and an assortment of brown sugars to produce a strong, light ale with a complex gamut of flavours.

Bridestones Brewing

Smithy Farm, Blackshaw Head, Hebden Bridge, HX7 7JB;
T: 01422 847104; E: info@bridestonesbrewing.co.uk;
W: www.bridestonesbrewing.co.uk

A dramatic outcrop of gritstone boulders above Todmorden, once the scene of pagan rites, lends its name to this family-owned brewery best known for its assertively citric best bitter **Pennine Gold** (4.3%). Malty session beer **Indian's Head** (3.7%) is named after another Pennine landmark; the fruity, floral Willamette hop exerts a presence in **American Pale Ale** (5%). The splendidly-titled New Delight Inn close to the Pennine Way is the brewery tap.

Bridlington Brewery

110 Quay Road, Bridlington, YO16 4JB

Local real ale favourites the Telegraph Inn and the Pack Horse are the ideal place to try beers from this microbrewery, established in the Telegraph's beer garden in 2014. Products include the zesty pale ale **Quay Gold** (4.2%) and steady-away brown ale **Jackdaw** (4%).

Bridge Brewery

Woodhead Rd, Holmbridge,
Holmfirth, HD9 2NQ;
T: 01484 687652;
E: manager@thebridgeholmbridge.co.uk;
W: www.thebridgeholmbridge.co.uk

An interesting trio makes up the regular output of a business symbiotic with the Old Bridge pub, Holmfirth's Brambles Wine Bar and a brewery farm where pigs feast on spent grain. **Blonde** (3.8%) is a nicely-balanced English pale bitter; companiable **American Pale Ale** (4%) has some moderate citric character, while the smooth **Vanilla Stout** (5.2%) is a sweet-talking soporific delight. The influence of New Zealand's remarkable hop-laden beer culture is evident in the Bridge's specials.

Bridgehouse Brewery

Hawkcliffe Works, Hebden Road, Oxenhope, BD22 9SY;
T: 01535 642893; E: info@bridgehousebrewery.co.uk;
W: www.bridgehousebrewery.co.uk

Smooth ruby ale **Bridgehouse Porter** (4.5%) is packed with toffee and malt flavours; golden **Holy Cow** (5.6%) has theatrical levels of juicy, fruity hop flavour.

Briggs Ales

Unit 1, Waterhouse Mill, 65-71 Lockwood Road,
Huddersfield, HD1 3QU;
T: 07427 668004; E: info@briggsales.co.uk;
W: www.briggssignatureales.weebly.com

Nick Briggs struck out on his own after a spell working for
Mallinsons (see p110), but continues to produce his own ales on
the Huddersfield plant.

    They include piney, red-berry flavoured **Techno** (4.2%), roasty,
cask-aged strong porter **Heavy Metal** (5.7%) and tropical fruit
golden ale **Hip Hop** (4.2%). **Mash Up** (3.9%) typifies Yorkshire's
"make do and mend" spirit by using hops left over from previous
brews. The exact recipe and strength will, of course, change
every time!

Briscoe's Brewery

16 Ash Grove, Otley, West Yorkshire, LS21 3EL; T: 01943 466515

Paul Briscoe put his doctorate in microbiology to good use in
establishing his eponymous three-barrel brewery producing ales like
the dry and bitter **Chevin Chaser** (4.3%) and hop-prominent **Otley
Gold** (3.9%).

    First brewed for an Otley engineering company, the substantial
Parker's Pet (6.1%) is a past champion at the Otley's beer festival –
quite an accolade given Otley's relentless thirst for great beer.

An Otley Pub Crawl

This busy market town on the southern edge of the Dales has long boasted an absolute wealth of public houses. There were once 30, and though a dozen of those have gone, it remains an absolute mecca for those in search of seriously good beer.

We'll start our circular tour at the town's bus station in Crossgate, where the **Old Cock**, with its rough-hewn oak beams, lintels and ancient stone fireplaces, has become an absolute star of the local scene, serving an ever-changing choice of real ales predominantly from local brewers. Etched mirrors and enamelled signs from ages past, advertising Tetley's Magnet Ales and Timothy Taylor Landlord, lend to the old alehouse feel.

Further along here is the sturdy, stone-fronted **Rose and Crown**, which attracts a slightly older crowd, and turn left into Bondgate to reach food and music venue **Korks** and the evergreen alehouse **The Junction**.

Retrace your steps along Bondgate to reach the **Bowling Green**, which was given a new lease of life by Wetherspoons, the **Otley Tavern** and then the **North Bar Social**, the furthest north of that pub group's chain. Around the corner in Kirkgate, the **Red Lion** and **Whitaker's** are a twosome popular with the locals, before we reach the stately, curved frontage of the 17th century **Black Horse**.

From here it's a short hop to the Market Place where there are the **Bay Horse** and **Black Bull** – reputedly drunk dry by Cromwell's troops, before they made similarly short work of the Royalists at Marston Moor. Further along in Boroughgate is the **Otley Tap House**, while Market Town Taverns' **Horse and Farrier** in Bridge Street is worthy of a short diversion too.

Selby pubs

The recent arrival of both Wetherspoon's **Giant Bellflower** in Gowthorpe, with its changing array of cask and keg ales, and the landmark freehouse **George Hotel** beside the Abbey, have brought a new dimension to a market town long-dominated by well-established traditional pubs like the **Nelson** in Ousegate, **Blackamoor** in Finkle Street and Sam Smiths' **Cricketers**, just across from the Abbey. **Selby Rugby Club** in Sandhill Lane serves some decent beer too. Outside the town, the **Wheatsheaf** at Burn, Selby – where I often used to drink after playing for Burn cricket club – **George and Dragon** at West Haddlesey, **Wadkin Arms** at Osgodby, **New Inn** at Cliffe and **Red Lion** at Kellington are all worth a visit. The lovely old **Chequers** at Ledsham, once hamstrung by archaic statute to six-day opening, now serves until 6pm on Sundays too.

Brown Cow Brewery

Brown Cow Road, Barlow, Selby, North Yorkshire YO8 8EH;
T: 01757 618947; E: susansimpson@browncowbrewery.co.uk;
W: www.browncowbrewery.co.uk

Almost 20 years of brewing earned Sue Simpson a prestigious award from Doncaster CAMRA in 2016 for exceptional services to real ale; she and partner Keith have established a solid reputation for their six-barrel plant from where they deliver beers within a 15-mile radius. Lager malt and American Cascade hops create the straw-pale **Sessions** (3.6%) which delivers some surprising citrus in the aftertaste; while there is more significant bitterness and depth of flavour to premium English ale **Over The Moon** (4.2%). But it is their darker beers, the coffee-ish premium dark mild **Captain Oates** (4.5%) and rich, slightly sweet **Mrs Simpson's Vanilla Porter** (5.1%) which have won a string of beer festival awards. Both are also available in bottle.

Burley Street Brewhouse

9 Burley Street, Leeds, LS3 1LD;
T: 07506 741039;
E: dawn@zigzaglighting.co.uk
www.burleystreetbrewhouse.co.uk

The one-bedroomed Rutland Hotel operated here from Victorian times. After a gas explosion wrecked the neighbouring shop it re-opened as the Fox and Newt, having expanded across the blast site. Brewing kit was first installed in the claustrophobic cellars in the 1980s and a string of licensees devoted varying levels of enthusiasm to the project. Its re-establishment as Burley Street Brewery in 2010 brought new continuity to the operation and the two regular beers have a healthy following in the pub upstairs and in its nearby sister pub the Pack Horse. They are blonde **Laguna Seca** (4%) whose gentle sweetness is followed by the grapefruity dryness of Chinook and First Gold hops; and traditional, well-balanced copper coloured best bitter **Brickyard** (3.8%).

Butcher's Dog Brewery

24 Middle Street South, Driffield, East
Yorkshire, YO25 6PS; T: 01377 254032;
E: info@thebutchersdog.co.uk;
W: www.thebutchersdog.co.uk

When former RAF technician Tim Waudby decided to turn his home brewing into a business, partner Nat's popular Driffield micropub the Brewer's Dog gave him a ready outlet for his produce. Black treacle gives extra substance to deep red **Peppa's Pawter** (4.7%); Cascade and Galaxy hops lend their citrus character to **Kukur IPA** (5.8%) while seven malts combine in the dry **Black Spot Stout** (4.6%).

Yorkshire's oldest pub

Just east of Leeds in Bardsey, the **Bingley Arms** is one of a very few pubs nationwide which can confidently claim to have a pre-conquest heritage. The pub's record list all the innkeepers since Samson Elys first began serving weary travellers on the road between Leeds and York in 953 AD.

Cap House Brewery

444 Victoria Works, Bradford Road,
Batley, WF17 5LW;
T: 01924 479909;
W: www.caphousebrewery.co.uk

Gary and Karen Wardman run the Reindeer Inn in Overton, which is the brewery tap for the beers produced by Gary and partner Peter Lister on a factory complex in nearby Batley. Cap House Colliery, now the National Mining Museum, is close by the Reindeer, and several beers draw on this proud subterranean heritage. You can certainly imagine sooted, work-weary colliers slaking their thirst on pints of the tangy, toffee-ish **Miners A Pint** (3.8%), or the brighter, sharper **Miner's Light** (4.2%) which is probably as close to a lager as any self-respecting Yorkshire pitman would ever dare venture. New Zealand's Nelson Sauvin hop lends white wine fruitiness to **Nelson IPA** (4.2%), while **North Pole** (4%), with its big blast of fresh orange, lemon and passion fruit, is one of a host of hearty Cap House blondes.

Captain Cook Brewery

White Swan, 1 West End, Stokesley, TS9 5BL;
T: 01642 710263;
E: mail@captaincookbrewery.com;
W: www.captaincookbrewery.com

Named after the famed local explorer, this brewery was established in 1999 in the 18th century White Swan pub and has now grown into a four-barrel plant whose cask and bottled beers are more widely available. They include the light and bitter **Slipway** (4%), and the dark, roasty, chocolatey **Black Porter** (4.4%). Firm, toffee-ish mild **Endeavour** (4.3%) honours Cook's most famous ship.

Chantry Brewery

Units 1-2 Callum Court, Gateway Industrial Estate, Parkgate, Rotherham, S62 6NR; T: 01709 711866; E: sean@chantrybrewery.co.uk; W: www.chantrybrewery.co.uk

The sad closure of Wentworth in 2016 left Chantry the only brewery in a town whose brewing history stretches back through companies like Bentley's and Mappin's who competed for custom among those who laboured in Rotherham's furnaces and glass factories. Fittingly, Sheffield steel was used to create this 20-barrel plant, from whence comes the pale and tangerine and vanilla-accented **Teaser** (4.5%), and the oily, toasty, **Special Reserve** (6.3%), an old ale packed with black treacle, raisins and suggestions of red wine. **Diamond Black** (4.5%) is a rich, full-bodied stout, while bright, crisp and refreshing **New York Pale** (3.9%), is a firm and crisp, refreshing sessionable golden ale whose name honours a local factory which once furnished the Big Apple with its distinctive red fire hydrants.

Sales of golden, zesty **Women of Steel** (3.9%) helped fund a bronze statue at Sheffield City Hall which honours women who worked in the steelworks during the world wars.

 The Cutlers' Arms, Westgate, Rotherham

A short walk from the football ground, this famous real ale pub blends old and new. Its name is an echo of the area's steel-making past; the Stones and Cannon brewery legends in the stonework and the stained glass remember a brewery long closed. Yet Chantry has given new life to the Cutlers, restoring its elegant features and giving customers an opportunity to once more try locally-brewed ales. With its high ceilings, red leather banquettes, deep green panelling and dark wallpaper, there is something re-assuringly traditional about this place, though the quality, microbrewed real ales – and even some new Chantry stained glass above the bar – bring it beautifully up to date.

Next door, the elegant old Alma stands in a state of sad disrepair just waiting for someone to offer the same loving care.

Concertina Brewery

Dolcliffe Rd, Mexborough S64 9AZ; T: 01709 580841

300 Great Beers To Try Before You Die is a best-selling bucket-list book by world-renowned beer writer Roger Protz; the third beer featured is from the tiny brewery below this private members' club. **Bengal Tiger** (4.6%) is a revelatory India Pale Ale, a traditional cask ale packed with the kind of extravagant rich fruit and spicy, resinous hoppy flavours so sought after by the new wave crafties.

The club itself – known locally as the Tina – dates back to the time when Mexborough's Concertina Band won prestigious prizes and played for Royalty.

It is the only members' club in the UK which brews on the premises; thankfully non-members are also made welcome.

Clark's Brewery

Westgate Brewery, Wakefield, West Yorkshire, WF2 9SW;
T: 01924 373328; E: jeff.hempsall@hbclark.co.uk;
W: www.hbclark.co.uk

H B Clark is the UK drinks trade's largest independent wholesaler, a business which continued uninterrupted during the 1960s and 70s when the explosion of keg beer saw production in their own brewery halted. A new micro-brewery resumed brewing in 1982 – and Clarks deliver their beers to pubs across the midlands and the north. Their flagship product is the interestingly spicy **Classic Blonde** (3.9%) while their new Merrie City craft beer marque has added **Atlantic Hop** (4%), **Cascadian** (4%), **Crystal Gold** (4.2%) and **Merrie Christmas** (4.3%) to the collection.

Right next door, and named after the brewery's founder, Henry Boon's is effectively the brewery tap and a perfect place to graze this selection.

A Wakefield pub crawl

The Westgate Run is perhaps Yorkshire's most notorious pub crawl. It takes drinkers to something like 20 bars and pubs and appeals to the stags, the hens and those who follow the herd.

This circular route from Westgate station, is based more on quality than quantity. Leaving the station, cross Westgate to find family-run alehouse the **Old Printworks** and traditional one-room boozer **Harry's Bar** side by side facing a car park. A little further up Westgate is Bank Street and the **Hop**, a tastefully refurbished home for live music and beers from Ossett Brewery (see p130). Continue towards the Cathedral spire, to reach the **Black Rock** in Cross Square, a famous largely unspoilt old Melbourne house which opened in 1842, and is the very first pub where I successfully ordered a pint, this rite of passage experience coming during a daring fifth form excursion into this den of adulthood.

Cross over into Bull Ring to reach understated cafe bar and beer shop the **Beer Exchange**, before heading east on Westmorland Street and taking a left on Vicarage Street to reach the famous Red Shed of **Wakefield Labour Club** – a bastion of socialism and real ale, and a symbolic contrast to the Trinity centre's temple of consumerism, right next door.

From here, head due south down Kirkgate to find the **Fernandes Brewery Tap** (p66), before a route march along George Street brings you to the **Bull and Fairhouse**, a city centre outpost for Great Heck brewery (p72). From here, Smyth Street brings you back to Westgate, and if you have chance for a last pint before your train, Clark's brewery tap **Henry Boons** is just beyond the station.

Beyond the city, the **Brewer's Pride** in Ossett, **King's Arms** in Heath and **Dunkirk Inn** in Denby Dale keep the real ale flame alight.

Copper Dragon Brewery

Snaygill Industrial Estate, Keighley Road, Skipton, BD23 2QR;
T: 01756 702130; E: info@copperdragon.uk.com;

Given their seemingly ubiquitous presence on bars across Yorkshire it feels as though Copper Dragon has been around for generations. But the Skipton Brewery was actually established as recently as 2002 and achieved its status as one of Yorkshire's fastest growing breweries largely through the soaraway success of Golden Pippin which remains the company's best-loved product, despite a recent change of ownership which has seen the brewery also being used to produce smaller-scale products under the Grey Hawk Brewery name.

The eye-catching logo of a fearsome dragon guarding a copper brewing vessel make these beers easy to spot, whether on a bar or on the supermarket shelves. Amber-coloured **Best Bitter** (3.8%) is a refreshing beer of genuine taste and substance with a rich sweet aroma and some genuine bitter bite in the finish but brewed to a moderate 4% ABV, which makes it eminently sessionable. Their firm and malty **Scott's 1816** (4.1%) and dark, smoky, complex **Broadwing Stout** (4.5%), brewed under the Grey Hawk label are others worth trying, whether on cask or in the bottle.

Crystalbrew

BAE Systems Business Park, Brough, HU15 1EQ

Undergoing something of a hiatus as we go to press, Crystalbrew will hopefully re-emerge later in 2017 following a change of ownership at the plant close to the Humber estuary.

 **Golden Pippin** (3.9%)

Originally introduced as a seasonal summer beer, Golden Pippin proved so popular that it was soon being brewed all year round. Whether in bottle or on draught, it's one of those "go-to" beers for drinkers seeking a reliable Yorkshire pale ale. It has the clear golden colour that the name suggests, and though it has only a moderate citric aroma, it bursts on the palate with a crisp, clean, tongue-cleansing burst of apple and gooseberry, before a long grapefruity aftertaste leaves you gagging for more.

COPPER DRAGON

GOLDEN PIPPIN

Daleside Brewery

Camwal Road, Starbeck, Harrogate, HG1 4PT;
T: 01423 880022;
E: enquiries@dalesidebrewery.com;
W: www.dalesidebrewery.com

Daleside was set up in 1988 by brewer Bill Witty at a time when micro-brewing was in its infancy, and many of the signs were suggesting that traditional British beer could be in terminal decline. Renowned writer and brewer Garrett Oliver, the founder of New York's trendsetting Brooklyn Brewery, learned the basics here. Bill died in 2007, but the brewery remains under the stewardship of his son Craig, and Daleside's draught ales continue to exert a significant presence both in the Dales and in Harrogate itself. They include the treacly **Daleside Bitter** (3.7%) and grapefruity **Daleside Blonde** (3.9%). Their strong dark bottled beers **Monkey Wrench** (5.3%) and **Morocco Ale** (5.5%) also have a keen following, while a partnership with Ripon Cathedral has spawned the perfectly potent **Ripon Jewel** (5.8%).

 **Old Leg Over** (4.1%)

There is something of the fruit and nut about this cheekily-named, bright and effervescent copper-coloured ale. The soft sweetness of dried fruit and almonds dominate a taste which is definitely more mild than bitter and deliciously easy drinking. Its malty, peaty nature develops further in the aftertaste and rather puts one in mind of a fine Scotch and in the mood for just a little more Leg Over.

The Grove, Holbeck, Leeds

A particular badge of honour for Daleside is that at the splendidly unspoiled Grove, a real ale paradise just south of Leeds city centre, their sessionable and citric Blonde is the only permanent real ale on the bar.

In recent years the Grove had its share of ups and downs – until Simon and Sharon Colgan added it to their little fold of pubs – the World's End in Knaresborough, Harrogate's lively Blues Bar (see p83) and Leeds music venue the Duck and Drake. With its musical heritage and long-standing commitment to real ale, the beautiful old Grove is a perfect fit. There has been a pub here since the 1830s, and the polished wood, tiling, stained glass and comfortable, utilitarian fittings speak of a bygone age.

Outside, everything has changed. Where once were factories, foundries and warehouses are now the media age businesses of Holbeck. The modest whitewashed brick of the Grove stands so close to the concrete sole of Bridgewater Place, it seems remarkable it hasn't simply been stamped out of existence.

Its musical heritage was key to its survival. Leeds Folk Club has met here since the sixties; Mark Knopfler founded the Notting Hill Billies over a few drinks in the back room; a French traditional music group rehearses here; Corinne Bailey-Rae occasionally performs unannounced on jam night. There's blues and bluegrass – and on "Open Mind Night" anything goes.

"People think you have to go to Dublin for this sort of thing," says Simon. "But it happens right here."

Dark Horse Brewery

Coonlands Laithe, Hetton, BD23 6LY;
T: 01756 730555; E:
richard@darkhorsebrewery.co.uk;
W: www.darkhorsebrewery.co.uk

Owner Richard Eyton-Jones already had some impressive breweries on his CV – Goose Eye and Old Mill in Yorkshire, St Peter's and Old Cannon in Suffolk – before he and wife Carole established Dark Horse Brewery in pretty Hetton in 2008, using their own borehole for water. And since 2016, their four beers **Hetton Pale** (4.2%), **Craven Bitter** (3.8%), **Night Jar** (4.2%) and **Blonde Beauty** (3.9%) have become permanently available. Hetton's renowned Angel Inn is perhaps the perfect place to sample these local brews, though they reach pubs across the Dales.

🍺 Hetton Pale Ale

This clean-tasting, slightly sweet and peachy 4.2% pale ale could hardly have had a more favourable introduction; its inaugural brew won the ITV series Yorkshire's Perfect Pint in 2008. Available both in bottle and cask, it continues to deliver on the uncomplicated values which took that prize. It pours an attractive golden colour with some seductive citrus in the aroma, before the deeper substance of malt and caramel emerge in the taste of a very easy-going Yorkshire ale.

 ## The Angel, Hetton

Just a half mile from the brewery, the stone-fronted Angel stretches out beside the road in this pretty little ribbon of a village just a few miles north of Skipton. Close by is Rylstone, home of the WI group which spawned the incredible Calendar Girls and a thousand low-rent imitations.

Like many Dales village pubs, the Angel remains a freehouse but has become the de-facto brewery tap for Dark Horse. Originally this was a 15th century drovers inn, where farmers would seek rest and refreshment – both for themselves and their animals – while driving them the many miles from their fields to market. The cattle may be long gone, but half a millennium on, this famous inn continues to offer valuable sustenance.

The Angel regularly features in lists of the very best dining pubs in the county and a visit to Pascal Watkins' beautiful, intimate restaurant with its gleaming glasses, glinting silver cutlery and crisp white linen tablecloths is always a treat. The nine beautifully-appointed bedrooms in restored outbuildings across the road mean that not only can you fully indulge on food and drink without the bothersome matter of a drive home afterwards but you can also cross back over for a hearty full English in the morning.

Doncaster Brewery

7 Young Street, Doncaster DN1 3EL;
T: 07921 970941;
E: doncasterbrewer@gmail.com;
W: www.doncasterbrewery.co.uk

The 2012 St Leger Festival was a
Classic start for the launch of a
brewery which was built from
scratch over the course of nine
months by engineer turned brewer
Ian Blaylock.

He runs it with wife Alison; both
are Donny born and bred and –
apart from regular appearances at
nearby festivals – their beers are
sold exclusively through their
excellent city centre tap, which also
boasts more than 50 European
bottled beers and a cracking wine
list. It was the town's CAMRA pub
of the year and Yorkshire's cider
pub of the year in 2016.

Each brew is named after
something related to Doncaster -
people, places, landmarks, historic
events – and even locomotives.
They include their surprisingly
carbonated caramelly **Sand House
Blonde** (3.8%) and the darker,
sturdier **Cheswold** (4.2%). These
are available in bottle, alongside
easy-going mild **Mansion House**
(3.6%) and dark, earthy, spicy
fireside ale **1194 Charter** (5.5%).

Seasonal offerings include the
Belgian-style pale ale **Town Fields**
(6.6%) and November's **Pumpkin
Porter** (4.6%).

A Doncaster Pub Crawl

The station is an appropriate place to begin a short real ale ramble around a town whose history is intertwined with that of the railways. Turn right from the entrance to reach West Street and the attractively tiled frontage of real ale and rock house the **Leopard**. Just around the corner in Sepulchre Gate is the **Corner Pin**, whose changing choice of local ales makes it a firm favourite with the local CAMRA branch.

From here, head north east along Cleveland Street to reach the **Doncaster Brewery Tap**, and just beyond it the idiosyncratic **Cask Corner** with its eight real ale handpumps. Continue in the same direction into Silver Street and Chantry brewery's **Flying Scotsman**, before heading back across town to Frenchgate and the narrow beam-fronted **White Swan**. From here head through, under or around the concrete bulk of the shopping centre, at which point you can decide whether to get back on your train or scurry into West Laith Gate for a swift one at the well-preserved inter-war **Plough** or Greene King's more formulaic **Tut and Shive** next door.

Eagles Crag Brewery

Unit 21, Robinwood Mill, Burnley Road, Todmorden, OL14 8HP;
T: 01706 810394; E: info@eaglescragbrewery.com;
W: www.eaglescragbrewery.com

An eight-barrel brewery which was named after a local landmark and based in an old mill designed by Sir Christopher Wren began its regular production in February 2017 based around a core range of four cask and bottled beers which are already permeating into pubs and bars either side of the Pennines.

Amber **The Eagle Has Landed** (4.6%) derives its notable piney and floral flavours from Cascade, Chinook and Simcoe hops, and is balanced with some rich malt; while the slightly less potent **Eye of The Eagle** (4.3%) is a touch more citric and has a resiny bitter finish.

Dark porter **The Eagle of Darkness** (5%) has some heady chocolate and coffee character, while **Golden Eagle** (4.7%) is a generously-proportioned sharply citrus American-hopped blonde bombshell.

Drinking in the heights

At 1,732 feet above sea level, the **Tan Hill Inn** in the Yorkshire Dales is the highest in the UK. Established in a bleak spot at the meeting point of Swaledale, Arkengarthdale and Bowes Moor in the 17th century, the pub remains a favourite with bikers, fell walkers – and particularly with those on the Pennine Way, which passes right beside here. With its sturdy stone frontage, exposed beams and roaring open fire, quality food and drink and warm hospitality it is the very essence of a Yorkshire country inn. On the third Thursday of the month it hosts the highest altitude open mic night in Britain, very possibly the world.

East Yorkshire Brewery

Unit 2A, Tokenspire Business Park, Beverley, HU17 0TB

This new brewery was in the process of starting production as this book went to press.

Elland Brewery

3-5 Heathfield Industrial Estate, Elland, HX5 9AE; T: 01422 377677;
E: info@ellandbrewery.co.uk; W: www.ellandbrewery.co.uk

Two microbreweries came together to establish Eastwood and Sanders in 2002 – and despite changes of ownership, location and personnel, it continues to do all the important things consistently well. Best known for its **1872 Porter**, CAMRA's Champion Beer of Britain in 2013, Elland also produces two citric pale ales, **Chinook** (3.9%) and **Beyond the Pale** (4.2%), fruity best bitter **Nettle Thrasher** (4.4%), soft and sessionable **Elland Blonde** (4%) and the slightly anaemic, spicy, wheat beer influenced **White Prussian** (3.9%).

1872 Porter

1872 was the year of the Mary Celeste, the first FA Cup Final – and the original recipe for this rich and treacly 6.5% porter. You know you are in for a treat as soon as you start to pour the beer, releasing some enticing caramelly aromas. Almost opaque jet black in the glass, it settles beneath a foaming ivory head, inviting you to dive in.

Once there, your palate is bathed in a silky blanket abundant in the luxurious array of flavours so redolent of a great porter. There is dark chocolate, the bitterness of espresso, soft malt, red wine and a smokiness which lingers in the top of the mouth as a final sweetness slowly develops on the throat. It's wonderful – and if you can ever find it in a wooden cask, drink the lot.

A Sheffield pub crawl

A city which has so warmly embraced the flourishing post-millennial culture of brewing is equally well served by its on-trade, providing for drinkers any number of rewarding pub crawls, whatever their thirst and stamina.

The **Riverside** in Kelham Island might be a good place to start, and from here it's a short hop to the excellent **Harlequin**, before proceeding towards the fleshpots of West Street by way of live music and continental beer paradise **Shakespeare's**. The **Three Tuns** is a couple of hundred yards due south from here, then a clutch of bars close to West Street in the west end of the city centre are funky gin bar **Old House**, foody **Red Deer** and the **Bath Hotel** – which like several in Sheffield is a bastion of Thornbridge, Derbyshire craft brewers par excellence. If you've a train to catch, head back to the station by way of the **Head of Steam** and quirky, arty **Rutland Arms**.

For those in the dramatically hilly Sheffield University student heartland an educational route might begin at restored Victorian alehouse **The Blake** in Blake Street, and continue by the **Closed Shop** in Commonside, with its beer garden and eight real ales and across the road to Thornbridge's lovely old stone-built **Hallamshire House**. From here it would be on to the **Punch Bowl** in Crookes for real ale and pizza while those with still more energy could expend it on a ramble to the foody and beautifully refurbished **York** in Broomhill, the **Fox and Duck**, where you can take your own food from nearby takeaways, and finish up at the **Doctor's Orders** in Glossop Road, voted Britain's best student pub in 2016 (see p105).

The **Kelham Island Tavern** (p28) and brewery taps the **Fat Cat** (p99), **Hilltop** (p88). **Sheffield Tap** (p163), **True North** (p171), **Regather** (p136) and **Sentinel** (p150) are each a perfect showcase for the city's ales.

Of suburban pubs, the **New Barrack Tavern** in Owlerton, **Broadfield** in Nether Edge, near neighbours the **Sheaf View** and **Brothers Arms** in Heeley, **Beerhouse** in Ecclesall Road and **Cremorne**, close to Sheffield United's ground, have each been recommended by local brewers as the ideal place to try their wares.

The **Coach and Horses** in Chapeltown, **Wisewood Inn** in Loxley, **Horse and Jockey** in Hillsborough, **British Oak** in Mosborough, **Travellers Rest** in Oughtibridge and **Norfolk Arms** alongside the busy A61 artery have each helped to renew the passion for real ale among those living on the fringes of the city.

Emmanuales

Unit 111, J C Albyn Complex, Burton Road, Sheffield, S3 8BT;
T: 0114 272 7256

Brewer Nick Law is spreading the good news, one beer at a time. Emmanuales began as a small-scale commercial brewery in the cellar of his terraced home, but in 2016 he up-scaled by moving in with Sheffield Brewing Company (see p152-153).

The brewery name and the motif of Christ on his bottles are no cynical gimmick; Nick has a strong Christian faith - and is keen to offer drinkers the heavenly experience of drinking "beers of biblical proportions". Four hop varieties are added one by one to the firmly bitter IPA **Oh Hoppy Day** (6.1%), while **Ryejoice** (5.4%) celebrates the holy matrimony of malted rye, Nelson Sauvin hops from New Zealand and Simcoe from Washington State.

Empire Brewing

The Old Boiler House, Unit 33, Upper Mills, Slaithwaite, HD7 5HA;
T: 01484 847343; E: empirebrewing@aol.com;
W: www.empirebrewing.com

The Beverley family's brewery began life more than a decade ago in a converted garage. They have since upped sticks to a picturesque canalside location from where they produce their thirst-quenching zesty session ale **Golden Warrior** (3.8%), rich, dark and dry **Porter** (4.7%), American-hopped pale ale **Strikes Back** (4%) and their citric, fruity New Zealand themed **Weka** (4.3%). My own favourite is the dark mild **Moonrakers** (3.8%) which combines a cocktail of ten different malts to create its luxuriant, chocolatey richness. They produce the house beer at the Commercial pub, and have recently installed a bottling line, both for their own beers and for other brewers chasing off-sales trade.

Exit 33 Brewing

Unit 7, 106 Fitzwalter Road, Sheffield, S2 2SP; T: 0114 270 9991;
E: office@exit33.beer; W: www.exit33.beer

The Harlequin on the north side of Sheffield City Centre is probably the ideal place to work your way through Exit 33's formidable range of ales which include the classic dark northern bitter **New England Best** (4.2%), easy-drinking German lager hopped **Blonde** (4%) and the rich, velvetty **Stout** (5%).

Several offer homage to the hops used in the brew, like the crisp, light, but big-tasting **Golden Cascade** (4.5%) and the uber-dry-hopped **Citra Smash** (6.5%), while **Two Tone** (4.6%) combines Citra and Mosaic – along with the energy and attitude of ska. **Nicaraguan Rum Cask Stout** (7%) is an imperial oat stout matured in wooden casks for a year, while hop-heavy Mosaic (4.1%), dazzlingly citric **Hop Monster** (4.5%) and subtle, multi-hopped **Hop Kiss** (3.9%) are also available in bottle.

Eyes Brewing

Leeds; E: info@eyesbrewing.com; W: www.eyesbrewing.com

Established in 2016, cuckoo brewer Eyes is the UK's first to be solely focussed on wheat beers, inspired by German tradition, modern innovation and long-forgotten English styles. Each brew contains at least 50 per cent wheat in the grist. I first came across **Kleine Weisse** (3.6%) at the Alfred bar in Meanwood and was surprised to find none of the haze and very little of the spicy character you would typically find with this style. Instead it proved a simple crisp, refreshing, golden bitter, though I expect those distinctive witbier characteristics are felt more forcefully in Eyes' **Hefeweizen** (5.2%), **Dunkelweisse** (5.2%) and **Hopfenweisse** (6%). A host of seasonals will draw still more variety from the wheaty theme.

Felix – see Junction

Fernandes Brewery

5 Avison Yard, Kirkgate, Wakefield, WF1 1UA;
T: 01924 291709;
E: brewery@ossett-brewery.co.uk; W: www.ossett-brewery.co.uk

When it was established as a brewpub in 1997, the exotic-sounding Fernandes was one of the early names in the vanguard of Yorkshire's brewing revolution, bringing to this former maltstore an exciting taste of things to come.

Although they are still on the same premises – where a lack of mains drainage means that all the waste water has to be manhandled to the drains – Fernandes has been owned by Ossett Brewery for a decade, providing them with a much broader reach for their beers, well beyond their taproom and Wakefield heartland.

Two of their dark beers, the dry and chocolatey **Malt Shovel Mild** (3.8%) and complex, sweet smoky stout **Black Voodoo** (5.1%) have garnered a string of awards, though their other regular beers – the pale and spicy **Centaur** (4.5%), smooth and sessionable **Ale To The Tsar** (4.1%) and robust roasted malt **Double Six** (6%) are also worth a try.

Mind you, with 90 different brews produced every year, Fernandes offers the curious drinker almost endless choice.

Frisky Bear Brewing

21 Weavers Close, Morley, LS27 9FF; W: www.friskybear.com

Home brewer Carl Saint established Frisky Bear in 2016. So far I've only managed to catch up with his American-style IPA **Grizzly Bear** (4.5%) where a rush of juicy fruit aroma heralds a taste big on fruity hop resins before a spicy, piney finish.

Five Towns Brewery

651 Leeds Road, Wakefield, WF1 2LU;
T: 07934 474180;
E: fivetownsbrewery@googlemail.com;
W: www.fivetownsbrewery.com

Recent expansion has enabled this 2.5 barrel brewery, based in a converted garage in Outwood, to brew three times a week – producing thirty nine-gallon casks of multi-award winning ale that has gained a following far beyond the five towns of Normanton, Pontefract, Featherstone, Castleford and Knottingley. The regular beers bring local dialect to the bar: **Owt L Do** (4.6%) is a rum-fortified mild, hefty stout, **Nowt** (6.7%) brims with roasted malt and coffee flavour, and prodigiously strong IPA **Summat Else** (7.2%) has a strong tropical fruit nose with gooseberry and maple syrup flavours. They don't skimp on the hops – even entry level pale **Mi Usual** (3.7%) features Nelson Sauvin, Comet and Citra while stronger session ale **Middle Un** (4.6%) dazzles with Perle Mosaic and Nelson Sauvin. A bewildering list of specials and seasonals refresh the range while a small quantity of each brew finds its way into bottle.

CHAPTER 1 · MADE IN BRITAIN · 4.9% ABV

fuggle bunny
BREW HOUSE
mad about hops

NEW BEGINNINGS
(AMBER BITTER)

Nose twitching, Fuggle peers from his den for the first time.

The fresh spring air is gently fragranced with aromas of **sweet honey and spice.** A breeze of **dry hoppiness** drifts by, whilst the warm glow of the sun gives the fields an **amber haze**...

Today was going to be a good day for an adventure...

CHAPTER 2 · MADE IN BRITAIN · 4.0% ABV

fuggle bunny
BREW HOUSE
mad about hops

COTTON TAIL
(PALE ALE)

Darting happily over the fields, Fuggle catches an unusual **aroma of lychees and citrus fruits**.

Intrigued, he follows his nose to a strange looking tree. Entwined around the large trunk were **5 different varieties of hops**. The branches bowed under the weight of ripe mixed fruits.

This was no normal tree!...

CHAPTER 7 · MADE IN BRITAIN · 5.0% ABV

fuggle bunny
BREW HOUSE
mad about hops

RUSSIAN RARE-BIT
(IMPERIAL BLACK STOUT)

Fuggles curiosity drove him on when surprisingly the temperature plummeted, Fuggle's breath formed **creamy** clouds. "Hello" said a voice like Velvet, an accent Fuggle did not recognise.

Suddenly through towering branches of **Pale Wheat** & **Dark Malt** a plume of **Coffee** and aromas of **Chocolate** revealed a dark sensual figure...sensational

Fuggle Bunny Brewhouse

1, Meadowbrook Park Industrial Estate, Halfway, Sheffield, S20 3PJ;
T: 07813 763347; E: wendy@fugglebunny.co.uk;
W: www.fugglebunny.co.uk

Fuggle Bunny's brilliant marketing strategy marries a story about an inquisitive rabbit to a catalogue of innovative quality beers, taking a quite radical new approach to getting noticed. Each new beer is a chapter, the ingredients the products of one bunny's search for excellence. The story starts with the malty, sweetish amber **New Beginnings** (4.9%) and progresses via the more markedly hoppy and citric **Cotton Tail** (4%) and the moderately bitter IPA **24 Carrot** (6%) – and more. As we went to press, Chapter 9, the American Pale Ale **La La Land** (3.9%) was about to launch, as was the first Fuggle Bunny pub.

Geeves Brewery

Grange Lane Industrial Estate, Carrwood Rd, Barnsley S71 5AS;
T: 07859 039259; W: www.geevesbrewery.co.uk

Home brews perfected on their houseboat formed the backbone of a commercial brewery established on an industrial estate west of Barnsley by Harry and Peter Geeves.

Six years on, and their core list includes **Topaz** (3.8%), a sessionable summery homage to this gently fruity Australian hop; oaky, coffee-ish, malty **Smokey Joe** stout (5%) and muscular IPA **Fully Laden** (6%). These are augmented by a host of interesting specials which include rich, sweet vanilla porter **Doughboy** (5.2%) and the decadent imperial stout **Nightmare** (8%). Its combination of full flavour and low alcohol saw **Rococo** (3.6%) named Sheffield's Champion Mild in 2014; attractive, eye-catching Geeves pump clips are a welcome sight on any bar.

Ghost Brew Co

Unit D, Tong Business Centre, Otley Road, Baildon, BD17 7QD;
T: 0113 418 2002; E: james@ghostbrew.co.uk; W: www.ghostbrew.co.uk

Having moved in with Baildon Brewery (see p16) this newcomer's beers are gradually making their way into both the off and on trade. Though the full-bodied texture gives a clue to its premium strength, amber **Banshee** (5.2%) is remarkably mellow and easy-going with moderate caramel and grapefruit character; deathly pale **Reaper** (4.4%) pulls off the opposite trick – though far less potent, it delivers sackfuls of grassy, resiny, citric hop. With its noticeable bubblegum aroma, the ghostly pale **Wraith** (3.8%) rattles biscuity malt and passion fruit along the corridors of the palate before slipping gently into the shadows with a dry, bitter finish. But through its stealthy, shadowy assault on the palate – significant peach and pine hop resins wrapped in a comfort blanket of toffee malt – the India Pale Ale **Phantom** (5.3%) is probably my favourite in the range. As the brewery's stylish website puts it, it's a super natural beer...

Golcar Brewery

60a Swallow Lane, Golcar, Huddersfield, HD7 4DX; T: 01484 644241;
E: golcarbrewery@btconnect.com

The Rose and Crown in Golcar is the ideal place to sample beers from a brewery which has been around for the best part of two decades, but whose capacity remains at just five barrels a week. The village west of Huddersfield is named after St Guthlac, an early Christian saint who preached here in Saxon times. His name is venerated in the full-bodied, big-tasting **Guthlacs Porter** (5%); other beers include a moderate strength trio – the delicately citric **Town End Bitter** (4%), roasted, sweetish **Golcar Dark Mild** (3.6%) and the floral, biscuity **Pennine Gold** (4%).

Golden Owl Brewery

Leeds; E: contact@goldenowlbrewery.co.uk

Always more cuckoo than owl, sightings of this fledgling brewery's products are now rarer than those of a Golden Eagle. The big fruity blast of Columbus and Galaxy hops in **Golden Owl Pale** (5.5%) promised plenty from this nest but one swallow doesn't make a summer. Hopefully they'll be back soon.

Goose Eye Brewery

Ingrow Bridge, South Street, Keighley, BD21 5AX; T: 01535 605807;
E: info@goose-eye-brewery.co.uk; W: www.goose-eye-brewery.co.uk

Three generations of the Atkinson family work at this popular Keighley Brewery which was one of the pioneering new-generation micros when it opened in 1991. Rooted in the traditional end of the market, their real ales include sessionable pale ale **Barm Pot** (3.8%), big-bodied orange-accented amber ale **Wonkey Donkey** (4.3%), roasted malt and chocolatey mild **Black Moor** (3.9%) and the big-bodied fruit and liquorice **Over and Stout** (5.2%). The massively hopped and grapefruity **Chinook** (4.2%) demonstrates a willingness to move with the times. It's their biggest seller.

Great Heck Brewery

Rosebank Cottage Brewery, Main Street, Great Heck, Goole, DN14 0BQ;
T: 01977 661430; E: steph@greatheckbrewery.co.uk;
W: www.greatheckbrewery.co.uk

Co-founder Denzil Vallance runs a brewery with a quirky attitude, determined independence and a decided preference for American hops. His website proclaims: "Each recipe is crafted by beer lovers, for beer lovers – accountants and marketeers don't get much of a look in."

Heaps of the finest English chocolate and crystal malts go into creating the dark and silky smooth session bitter **Dave** (3.8%) while **Amish Mash** (4.7%) fuses German Weizen yeast and American IPA hops to create a cloudy wheat beer with more citrus and banana than your average greengrocers.

Other beers include pale thirst-quencher **Mercy** (4%), dark IPA **Black Jesus** (6.5%) and aromatic **Citra** (4.5%) which is a showcase for this dazzling American hop.

Several are available in bottle.

🍺 Yakima IPA (7.4%)

Great Heck this is a strong beer! Named after the Washington State valley which provides the hops for this sweet, rich-textured, chestnut brown ale, Yakima is Denzil's super strength IPA. The aroma is surprisingly understated, but the beer really announces itself with a blast of toffee and blackberries on the palate, which develops into a really long dry aftertaste.

Great Newsome Brewery

Great Newsome Farm, South Frodingham, Winestead, Hull, nr HU12 0NR;
T: 01964 612201; E: enquiries@greatnewsomebrewery.co.uk;
W: www.greatnewsomebrewery.co.uk

Four generations of the Hodgson family have farmed the rich soil of Holderness, roughly half way between the suburbs of Hull and the bracing, windswept, shifting spit of the Spurn coast. They diversified into brewing a decade ago and have since garnered an enviable reputation for beers such as the pale and refreshing **Sleck Dust** (3.8%), the saffron-rich **Jem's Stout** (4.3%) and the easy-drinking malty chestnut ale **Ploughman's Pride** (4.2%).

Honouring the local dialect name for a hedgehog, **Pricky Back Otchan** (4.2%) is a lemony, nutty, butterscotchy ale whose significant substance lends the impression of a beer a good deal more potent. Further beers under the Brewculture name were introduced in 2017 to mark Hull's year as City of Culture.

🍺 Frothingham Best (4.3%)

I found bottles of Frothingham Best on offer in my local branch of Co-Op alongside a number of other Yorkshire ales on a three-for-a-fiver deal. Which is great value when you consider that not long ago, Frothingham Best beat all comers from around the globe to pick up first prize at the World Beer Awards – the brewing equivalent of the Oscars. Once I renewed my acquaintance with this fine best bitter, it was not hard to imagine why. Frothingham Best pours an attractive amber colour, with a gentle enticing biscuity aroma and an appropriately frothing head. Once on the palate, this beer's lavish, silky nature distributes warming malt and the bitterness of berries and green apples in roughly equal measure.

Great Yorkshire Brewery

Main Street, Cropton, YO18 8HH;
T: 01751 417330;
E: info@newinncropton.co.uk;
W: www.thegreatyorkshirebrewery.co.uk

Beer has been brewed in this moors village since before the Civil War and in recent decades, Cropton Brewery became a Yorkshire legend, producing from a microbrewery behind the New Inn a host of fabulous beers – favourites like King Billy Bitter and Monkman's Slaughter – which could be enjoyed either in the brewery tap, or further afield.

A recent re-branding, has seen the brewery renamed as Great Yorkshire, while whippets, cricket bats and a pigeon have become appropriate motifs on the label. Few beers from the previous roster have survived into the brewery's new guise. Instead, gently bitter and thirst-quenching **Yorkshire Pale** (3.8%) is a bright deep gold with a determined creamy head, a soft and understated aroma and a nicely balanced taste that boasts just a suggestion of gooseberry. Pale and piney **Yorkshire Lager** (4.2%) delivers more firmness, bitterness and substance than some mainstream 5% continental lagers can offer. **Blackout** (5%) is a rich and velvety, chocolate stout. The brewery runs daily tours.

The New Inn, Cropton

The New Inn has plenty more to recommend it, beyond simply being the tap for the Great Yorkshire Brewery next door. There's quality, locally-sourced food which can either be taken in the bar or its more formal restaurant, a spacious downstairs function room and a conservatory which overlooks the well-kept beer garden.

As befits a bustling stone country pub on the edge of North York Moors National Park, the décor is clean and functional to withstand the relentless footfall of all types of clientele – from hiking booted explorers to casual day trippers. There's exposed stone pillars, wood in abundance and lots of comfortable seating.

It's not even as though you need to travel far at closing time: there are nine smartly-appointed rooms, a self-contained cottage and even a campsite for those who prefer to explore a closer relationship with nature.

Greyhawk – see Copper Dragon

Half Moon Brewery

Forge House, Ellerton,
York YO42 4PB;
T: 01757 288977;
E: info@halfmoonbrewery.co.uk;
W: www.halfmoonbrewery.co.uk

Tony Rogers worked in engineering and IT for many years, while quietly honing his skills as a home brewer. Now, behind sage green garage doors in this cul-de-sac village south of York, and using tanks salvaged from a shampoo factory, his five-barrel brewery produces an interesting choice of beers which are distributed across Yorkshire, both in cask and bottle.

Until 1969, this was the blacksmith's workshop, a fact honoured by bright amber softly spiced and lemony **Old Forge Bitter** (3.8%). American Cascade hops lend a significant blast of grapefruit to **F'Hops Sake** (3.9%), while Bramling Cross adds dark berry notes and a rounded, fruity bitterness to **Blonde** (4.2%).

Seasonal beers **Lunar IPA** (5.5%), **Robustus Lunam** stout (5%) and the elderflower-infused **Midsummer** (3.6%) play to the lunar theme.

The excellent tours run from York railway station by brewtowntours.co.uk bring a stream of new visitors to Half Moon, where they are treated to some innovative beer and food match-ups.

🍺 Dark Masquerade (3.6%)

Despite its rather moderate strength, this full-bodied brown ale is a robust cocktail of dark chocolate, cloves, bitter orange marmalade and liquorice. The aroma is not unlike that of a wheat beer and there's something of that clovey, banana experience on the palate, before some earthy bitterness and interesting smoky notes emerge in the finish. On a recent visit to Half Moon's tiny taproom the beer was being imaginatively served with segments of Terry's Chocolate Orange – a good match. Dark Masquerade is a two-time winner in the Mild Category of the SIBA North East Awards.

Halifax pub crawl

A short wander around Halifax town centre brings you to three pubs very much of their own time. First there's the Edwardian listed **Gundog** in Crown Street, then the **Victorian Craft Beer Cafe** in Powell Street, a bold new use of an old building, then the Ossett Brewery-owned art deco gem the **Three Pigeons**, close to Shay Stadium.

A little beyond the town centre are the **Cross Keys** in Siddal, **Big Six** free house in Savile Park and the foody **1904**, which is hidden away under a concrete viaduct on the town's eastern approaches.

A mile or so east of the town is the beautiful old **Shibden Mill** beside Red Beck which once drove the waterwheel which gives this quality gastropub pub its name. Also worth a visit are the **Golden Fleece** in Bradshaw Lane, north of the town, and the **Spring Rock** and **Dog and Partridge** to the south.

Elland's canalside **Barge and Barrel**, Brighouse's **Beck** and Rastrick's **Round Hill** have each been recommended by breweries featured in this book.

Halifax Steam Brewery

Southedge Works,
Hipperholme, Halifax, HX3 8EF;
T: 07506 022504;
E: info@halifax-steam.co.uk;
W: www.halifax-steam.co.uk

Based in Hipperholme, just east of Halifax, this five-barrel plant produces a changing range of beers which are predominantly sold through the Cock O' The North pub on the same site. **Uncle Jon** (4.3%) is a nicely rounded, malty brown ale.

The Shibden Mill Inn

Specialist beer shops

The extraordinary popularity of beer has been felt way beyond the on-licence trade. It has also helped underpin the development of a series of specialist beer stores, whose range and expertise comfortably outstrips the off-licence chains and even the most beer-committed supermarket. Sheffield has at least three – **Beer Central**, **Hop Hideout** and **Turners**, while in Leeds there are the **Little Leeds Beer House**, **Beer Ritz** and **Raynville Superstore**, which is an unassuming suburban corner stop, with a fabulous selection of beers. Others worth checking out include **Bier Huis** in Ossett, **Fuggles** in Ilkley, **Curious Hop** in Otley, **Arcade** in Huddersfield, **House of the Trembling Madness** in York (see p37), **Drinks Well** in Ripon, **Yorkshire Ales** in Goole and **Jug and Bottle** in Bubwith. This isn't a comprehensive list; there are plenty more.

Hambleton Ales

Melmerby Green Rd, Melmerby, Ripon, HG4 5NB; T: 01765 640108;
E: office@hambletonales.co.uk; W: www.hambletonales.co.uk

The famous White Horse of Kilburn is the emblem of this trailblazing brewery established by Nick Stafford in 1991 and the equine theme continues into beers such as the **Stallion Amber** (4.2%) and **Stud Blonde** (4.3%). The aptly-named **Nightmare Porter** (5%) came about when he began a new brew one morning only to realise that he didn't have all the ingredients. Even so, the creamy, chocolatey porter he cobbled together wasn't bad – it was the first winner of CAMRA's Winter Champion Beer of Britain award and remains one of his best-known beers. As commercial director of SIBA, Nick has helped to bring a host of other small brewers into the marketplace; the Melmerby brewery has a small-scale bottling line used by other small breweries across Yorkshire and beyond.

Hamelsworde Brewery

41B Kirkby Rd, Hemsworth, WF9 4BA; T: 07530 669332;
E: hamelsworde@live.co.uk; W: www.hamelsworde.co.uk

Christened with the Saxon name for Hemsworth, Hamelsworde is the brainchild of Dan Jones, who turned a 15-year home-brew hobby into a business. Beers include the jet black and liquorice-accented **Spanish Stout** (4.2%), the dark, substantial nutty brown ale **Colin Brown** (5.2%), and the orangey wheat beer **Scalded Shoulder** (5.2%), so named because of an injury Dan suffered in its creation. Fresh amber ale **Haley's Comet** (4.5%) has some citric zest and an effervescence which distributes solid hop bitterness right across the palate. A brewery tap opened in 2015; its six handpumps provide a perfect opportunity to browse the lot.

Harrogate pub crawl

A few years ago, you might have struggled to find a really good beer house in the centre of Harrogate. While nearby Knaresborough had several – not least the evergreen **Blind Jack's** – the well-to-do spa town was more focussed on restaurants and wine bars, with the pub trade mostly dominated by national bar chains.

This little crawl shows just how much that has changed. It starts in the **Harrogate Tap**, which is in one of the town's original railway buildings and can be accessed either from Station Parade or directly from the platform. It's part of the Tapped group (see p162) and though they don't brew here, you can expect the same eclectic choice.

Walk down past the bus station and turn left into Cheltenham Parade and towards the bottom of the hill you'll find the simple,

Harrogate Brewing Co

41 Claro Court Business Centre, Harrogate, HG1 4BA;
T: 07774 891664; E: info@harrogatebrewery.co.uk;
W: www.harrogatebrewery.co.uk

Powerful, barrel-aged **Kursaal Imperial Stout** (7.5%) is the outstanding performer from this one-man-band brewery, whose railway-inspired livery is a regular sight in the spa town's pubs and bars. The beers include zingy **Cold Bath Gold** (4.4%) and mysterious, sulphurous **Horse Head Stetson** (5.9 %). Fresh and summery **Pinewoods Pale** (4.4%) is also available in bottle.

Hedonism central – The Blues Bar

sociable **Little Ale House** micropub where casks are racked up in glass-fronted cabinets.

From here, a couple of left turns and a short trek up Parliament Street brings you to **The Winter Gardens** – an amazing conversion of this elegant building into a pub and restaurant. As Wetherspoon bars go, this one is a cut above. Further up the hill, turn into The Ginnel, where there's a focus on Yorkshire ales, both craft and keg, and quality pizzas at **Major Tom's**.

Continue towards the historic Pump Rooms, the fashionable heart of Harrogate's Victorian tourist trade. Just beyond here is the newly-refurbished **Old Bell Tavern,** which preserves the memory of Farrah's world-famous Harrogate Toffee which was once made here. Further along Cold Bath Road – even the street names here are something special – is the well-kept **Fat Badger,** a modern take on the traditional city tavern.

Though this pub crawl offers opportunities for detours, such as to the nicely preserved **Coach and Horses** alongside the lush town centre acres of the Stray at West Park or to **10 Devonshire Place**, a Georgian coaching house now re-invented as an ale and gin paradise, there really is only one place to end your pub crawl. Just along Montpellier Parade is the lively, hedonistic **Blues Bar**, with its great beer, funky food, and a regular programme of live music. For exuberant, effervescent, sheer wild times, it's hard to beat.

Harthill Village Brewery

The Paddocks, 6 Union Street, Harthill, Sheffield, S26 7YH; T: 07736 246474

This five-barrel brewery is the most southerly in Yorkshire; the name lends itself to profuse punning pumpclips. Velvety **Dark Hart Festival Reserve** (6.5%) with its spicy dark fruit notes is a high-octane version of the toffee-biscuity **Dark Hart** (5%). Australian Galaxy and American Cascade hops provide weighty citrus characteristics to blonde **Hart Stopper** (4%); **Warm Harted** (4.4%), with its oat malt, black treacle and ginger is liquid parkin.

Hedge Row Brewing

Heaton, Bradford; T: 07714435599; E: hedgerowbrewingco@gmail.com

24-year-old Michael Coffey established this new brewery behind his home in Heaton in 2016. The lightly-spoken, slightly flowery, sessionable bright straw-coloured **Daisy Hill Blonde** (4%) was quite a hit at Leeds Beer Festival in 2017.

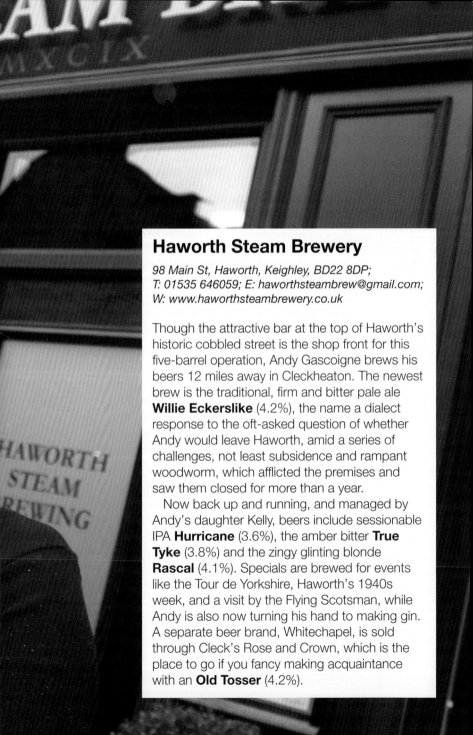

Haworth Steam Brewery

98 Main St, Haworth, Keighley, BD22 8DP;
T: 01535 646059; E: haworthsteambrew@gmail.com;
W: www.haworthsteambrewery.co.uk

Though the attractive bar at the top of Haworth's historic cobbled street is the shop front for this five-barrel operation, Andy Gascoigne brews his beers 12 miles away in Cleckheaton. The newest brew is the traditional, firm and bitter pale ale **Willie Eckerslike** (4.2%), the name a dialect response to the oft-asked question of whether Andy would leave Haworth, amid a series of challenges, not least subsidence and rampant woodworm, which afflicted the premises and saw them closed for more than a year.

Now back up and running, and managed by Andy's daughter Kelly, beers include sessionable IPA **Hurricane** (3.6%), the amber bitter **True Tyke** (3.8%) and the zingy glinting blonde **Rascal** (4.1%). Specials are brewed for events like the Tour de Yorkshire, Haworth's 1940s week, and a visit by the Flying Scotsman, while Andy is also now turning his hand to making gin. A separate beer brand, Whitechapel, is sold through Cleck's Rose and Crown, which is the place to go if you fancy making acquaintance with an **Old Tosser** (4.2%).

Helmsley Brewing Co

18 Bridge St, Helmsley, York, YO62 5DX; T: 01439 771014;
E: beer@helmsleybrewingco.co.uk; W: www.helmsleybrewingco.co.uk

An on-site bar and shop attracts a steady stream of visitors to a brewery which opened in 2014 and is already a favourite in the pubs of the old North Riding.

Chestnut-coloured **Yorkshire Legend** (3.8%) blends five local malts into a toasty, caramelly Yorkshire bitter, while **Howardian Gold** (4.2%) bursts with zesty lemon and tangy hop notes. Luxurious tropical fruit IPA **HiPA!** (5.5%) was developed during a spell brewing at the University of California and **Santa's Little Brewer** (5%) is an interesting mulled stout for the Christmas market.

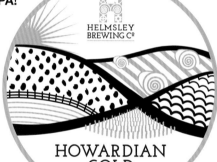

Dry golden bitter **Striding the Riding** (4%) is the official beer of the Cleveland Way and includes a blend of four hops from three different countries. I came across it by chance during an afternoon visit to the Forresters Arms, below the chalk landmark of the white horse in Kilburn, which is one of the early pub stops in the 110-mile scenic trek through the national park and down the Yorkshire coast. The brewery makes a donation for every firkin purchased.

🍺 Helmsley Honey (4.5%)

English, Australian and Slovenian hops are blended into this attractive golden ale. But it is the honey which dominates, both in the floral aroma and in the graceful, luxurious taste. Two different wild flower and heather honeys are used in the brew, both sourced from the North York Moors National Park. Like many of the Helmsley beers, this is available in both cask and bottle.

Here Be Monsters Brewery

Holmfirth; T: 07792 174863; E: info@monsterbeer.co.uk;
W: www.monsterbeer.co.uk

With brewer Doug Scard currently brewing on a 200-litre plant, sales from his curiously-named brewery have been largely concentrated on Holmfirth and nearby Huddersfield. But he's currently in the process of upscaling the operation; a 1,000-litre brewkit would give his products a wider reach.

They include coffee-and-blackcurranty **Dark Fury** (4.9%), a series of different **Cyclops** (4.4%) ales which each showcase the nature of single hop varieties, and the disarmingly sweet Belgian brown ale **Bokkenrider** (4%). The zesty, marmaladey nature of **Blonde Fury** (4.9%) seems rather at odds with its description as an English IPA – but it's worth a try all the same.

Hilltop Brewing

Sheffield Rd, Conisbrough, Doncaster DN12 2AY; T: 01709 868811

The Hilltop Hotel has been a real ale favourite for some years now; the recent addition of a brewhouse in the rear yard was a logical next step. The hotel is the obvious place to try the produce, though they have begun to make their way further afield. They include a gentle and easy-going **Blonde** (4%), a light and faintly agricultural **IPA** (5%) and a smooth and interesting winter warming **Bourbon Stout** (5%).

Horbury

The Toppits, Healey Road, Ossett, WF5 8LN

Founded on a one-barrel plant in 2016, Horbury has since decamped to a larger plant at the Brewers Pride pub in Ossett. Beers include golden **First Light** (4.1%), as uncomplicated as the brewery's minimalist pump clips, and the more noticeably citric **Sundown** (5.2%).

The Hop Studio

3, Handley Park, Elvington,
York, YO41 4AR;
T: 01904 608029;
E: hello@thehopstudio.com;
W: www.thehopstudio.com

Though it features just two regular beers – the citric **Pale** (4%) which draws heavily on the influence of New Zealand hops and the luscious vanilla-accented **Porter** (4.3%) – this innovative brewery has gained in virtually no time a stellar reputation. A year-round bottling operation has brought to market some really confident ales; for me the very best are the dark ones such as the roasted, brandy-ish dark chocolate stout **Chocolat** (6.5%) and the deeply soporific, dark fruit and sherry-influenced **Rievaulx** (10%), brewer Dave Shaw's Yorkshire interpretation of Belgium's super-strong Quadrupel style.

Brewer Dave Shaw shows off Treason, a porter brewed specially for sale in Parliament.

Hop and coming

New breweries are coming into the scene all the time, and as this book went to press I learned that a new brewery called **Little Shed** had been established at the Pax Inn at Thorp Arch. I also have high hopes for the curiously-named **Iron Rabbit** brewery based in South Leeds, which is very small scale but hoping to start commercial brewing soon.

Hungry Bear

10-14 Stonegate Rd, Leeds, LS6 4HY; T: 0113 274 0241;
E: thehungrybeer@gmail.com; W: www.thehungrybear.co.uk

Leeds's most under-rated, under-stated brewery sits above a little bar and restaurant in Meanwood, where brewer Phil Marsh has been creating interesting small-volume brews exclusively for his own customers since 2013. His bottled beers are dispensed in simple swing-top bottles without even the luxury of a label, a tiny luggage tag typed with the name of the beer and its strength allows you to know what you're drinking, before a firm push at the metal hinge releases the ceramic stopper in satisfying fashion. Flaxen, full-bodied, effervescent **West Coast IPA** (7.2%) has an aroma of tart green apples, and on the palate there's sweet pineapple and bitter grapefruit. The murmuring sweetness of vanilla dominates the aroma of jet black **Vanilla Bourbon Porter** (6.3%) but this soon gives way to silky smooth, dark bitter chocolate on the palate, dying away with dusty dryness on the back of the throat.

A recent development has seen the bar serve draught beer for the first time – each one fresh, unfiltered and unpasteurised. They include sessionable pale ale **Golden Lark** (3.8%) and the more substantial **Meanwood Pale** (5.6%) but with each brew being little more than 70 litres, the choice varies daily.

Ilkley Brewery

Ashlands Road, Ilkley, LS29 8JT; T: 01943 604604;
E: maryjane@ilkleybrewery.co.uk; W: www.ilkleybrewery.co.uk

The original Ilkley Brewery and Aerated Water Company was formed in 1873, but was swallowed up by Bass and stopped producing in 1920. It wasn't until 2009 that brewing returned to the town, since when Ilkley Brewery has developed a solid reputation founded on the excellent session pale ale **Mary Jane** (3.5%) named after one of the protagonists of famous folk song Ilkley Moor Baht 'at. But Ilkley have produced well over 100 different ales in that time and feature on the shelves of most of the major supermarkets. Many are American-influenced, like New World influenced **Ilkley Pale** (4.2%), amber **Rombald** (4.5%) and west coast IPA **Crossroads** (5.4%). Others include rich and emollient oatmeal stout **Hanging Stone** (5%), coffee milk stout **Holy Cow** (4%) the devilishly spicy and chocolatey chipotle stout **Mayan** (6.5%) and **Barbarossa** (5%), a spicy, blackcurranty ale with the telling influence of southern hemisphere hops.

🍺 Siberia (5.9%)

Ilkley's penchant for experimentation is well illustrated by this crisp, fruity ale that combines Belgian styling with Yorkshire rhubarb and hops from the USA and central Europe. Rhubarb is a local delicacy of course; some unfeasibly high percentage of the world's output of this fruit-hyphen-vegetable is grown in the nine-square-mile triangle between Wakefield, Morley and Rothwell. Added at fermentation, it delivers to the beer an unmistakable sourness, not unlike the dry refreshing nature of a Belgian Saison, traditionally brewed in winter time and stored to slake the thirst of farmworkers in summer. This beer has some cider-like characteristics, an appley nose and some determined carbonation.

Imperial Club Brewery

Cliff Street, Mexborough S64 9HU; T: 01709 584000;
E: imperialclub@hotmail.co.uk

The lively Imperial Club just outside the centre of Mexborough is the tap for this micro-brewery and well worth a visit. It's a simple, wide-open beer hall with a stage at one end and a bar at the other; an array of musical instruments hang from the ceiling while vintage rock posters jostle for space with pumpclips above the bar. Alongside three guest ales, four of the Imperial brews were available on my visit. For me, the best was the dark, smooth and slightly treacly, traditional Yorkshire ale **Classical Bitter** (3.6%). There are some admirable warming, mellow, fruity notes to the blonde ale **Nah Then** (4.5%), while the super pale **Platinum Blonde** (4%) has more of the sharp, refreshing, citric nature that its colour suggests. **Stout Wi Nowt Tekken Out** (6%) is a high octane, dark and dangerous beast.

Isaac Poad Brewing

Axholme Croft, Chapel St, Cattal, York YO26 8DY;
T: 01423 358114;
E: beer@isaacpoad.co.uk;
W: www.isaacpoadbrewing.co.uk

Grain traders for more than a century and a half, Isaac Poad diversified into beer in 2016, building on long-established local connections to source their materials; aside from the hops, everything is grown in Yorkshire. Currently brewing their moderate-strength cask and bottled ales at Wold Top (see p180), they hope to have their own brew kit operational by the end of 2017. The numbers in their beer names echo their long history – the year of foundation, the company's previous addresses. **Number 84** (4.5%) is a crisp, floral IPA whose citric attack steals stealthily across the palate; golden **Number 86** (3.6%) manages to ally moderate strength with significant body; deep amber and nutty best bitter **1863** (3.8%) stirs warm memories of high-watermark Tetley Bitter from the old Leeds brewery. "Our remit is to produce traditional Yorkshire session ales," brewery manager Chris Dearnley tells me. "That's an art which has been lost in this rush towards mega-hops and premium strength."

James & Kirkman Brewery

4 Wakefield Road, Pontefract, WF8 4HN; T: 07590 265381;
E: jamesandkirkmanbrewery@gmail.com;
W: www.jamesandkirkmanbrewery.com

David James founded Fernandes Brewery and also owned the East Coast brewery in Filey before establishing James & Kirkman in 2013. At each of these, his standout recipe has been the multi award-winning and surprisingly well-balanced **Empress of India** (6%) whose typical new-wave IPA tropical fruit flavours are anchored to a malty, slightly sweet backbone. **Stallion** (3.8%) is a dark and malty best bitter, **Miner's Mild** (3.6%) a soft gentle mild with some smoky undertones, delicate **New American Pale** (4.4%) less distinctly citric than the name suggests. Their pump clips, featuring simplistic line drawings on a yellow background, are easy to spot on any bar.

John Smith's Brewery

The Brewery, Tadcaster,
LS24 9SA;
T: 01937 832091;
E: customerservices
    @johnsmiths.co.uk;
W: www.johnsmiths.co.uk

The Tadcaster Brewery was founded in 1758 and bought around a century later by John Smith, who later moved his business next door, gifting the old brewery to his nephew Samuel Smith.

Now owned by Heineken, the brewery's traditional Yorkshire Squares have been replaced by conical steel fermenters producing just keg **John Smith's** (3.6%) which is an uncomplicated brew of moderate malt and minimal hop character. It has been the biggest selling bitter in the United Kingdom since the mid-1990s.

With a capacity of around 3.8m hectolitres, John Smith's is one of the biggest breweries in the UK – and also produces international brands including **Newcastle Brown** (4.7%), **Fosters** (4%), **Kronenbourg** (5%) and **Amstel** (4.1%).

A Barnsley pub crawl

Three of Barnsley's best pubs are within 100 yards of each other. New micropub the **Arcade Alehouse** is based in a former cake shop in the town's Victorian Arcade. Close by here in Market Hill are the **Old No 7**, a perfect place to survey the Acorn Brewery range (p6), and Wetherspoon's **Joseph Bramah**. Travel south along Market Street to reach the coal-themed **Silkstone**. Beyond the town centre, to the south east is the **Dove**, a local showcase for Snaith's Old Mill brewery (p126), to the north west the family-owned, family-friendly **Commercial**.

The Jolly Boys' Brewery

Redbrook Business Park, Wilthorpe Road, Barnsley, South Yorkshire, S75 1JN; T: 07900 403206; E: brewers@jollyboys-brewery.co.uk; W: www.jollyboys-brewery.co.uk

Some of the best conversations take place in pubs. The Jolly Boys' Brewery was established in a Scarborough snug where four friends, all of them educators, realised that this was something they wanted to pursue. One of the four, Hywel Roberts, takes up the story: "The Jolly Boys have all spent their working lives contributing via their day jobs to the support of others in society. This moral drive is important to us. Couple this with a love of beer, respect for community and pride in doing a good job, we made a life-changing decision: we were going to brew beer. What more honourable and worthwhile calling could there be? If The Jolly Boys' Brewery were a person, he'd be a listener, a carer, a mood-lifter, honest and true. He'd be non-bureaucratic and free-spirited. He'd also get a round in."

With brewing having only started recently, their efforts are concentrated on a familiar triptych of recipes – **Jolly Blonde** (4%), **Jolly Boys' Golden Best** (4.5%) and **Jolly Collier Porter** (5%) – but the boys are ambitious to grow the sweep and span of their ales.

Jolly Sailor Brewery

77 Barlby Road, Selby, YO8 5AB;
T: 01757 707564;
E: jollysailorbrewery@gmail.com;
W: www.jollysailorbrewery.uk

I'm long overdue a visit to the excellent Jolly Sailor in Cawood for my pub column in the Yorkshire Evening Post. I came here a few years ago and chanced upon a great pub quiz, but this was long before they started brewing their own beer.

Brewing began in 2012, not in Cawood itself but actually based some five miles away in an old boxing club behind the Olympia Hotel on the outskirts of Selby. Both pubs stock the beers, as does the Drax Sports and Social Club.

They include four regular ales: **Jolly Blonde** (3.8%) is an easy-going and fruity refresher, while **Cue Brew** (4%) is a jet black mild and **Jolly Gold** (3.9%) has some interesting herbal notes. The quality pale ale **Bullseye** (3.8%) picked up top prize in the Pale and Amber Beer category at 2016's York Beer Festival.

Their catalogue expands through occasional and seasonal beers, such as light and zesty **Jolly Spring** (4.3%), and the creamy, coffee-tinged **Jolly Dark Nights** (5%) is definitely one to try.

Three of the regular ales are also available in bottle.

Junction Brewpub

1 Baildon Rd, Baildon, Shipley BD17 6AB; T: 01274 582009

For drinkers who like to choose on the basis of colour, Junction's names offer an easy guide. Brewed primarily for the pub upstairs, they include significantly-hopped **Blonde** (4%), sweetish porter **Dark Thoughts** (4.6%) and fruity **Golden Splendour** (3.8%). A number of brews are also created under the Felix brand, including the golden **Boothtown Blonde** (3.9%).

Just the Ticket – see Settle

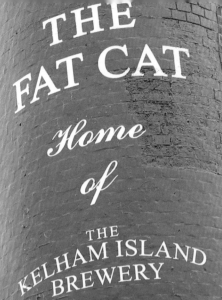

Kelham Island Brewery

23 Alma Street, Sheffield, S3 8SA; T: 0114 249 4804;
E: sales@kelhambrewery.co.uk; W: www.kelhambrewery.co.uk

The Fat Cat in Alma Street remains the perfect place to make acquaintance with Kelham Island Brewery, which was established by academic Dave Wickett in the beer garden in 1990. Right now, new breweries open all the time, trading on the huge popularity of beer; back then it was a more speculative venture and the city's first new independent brewery in almost a century. A pub which looks quite small from the outside has plenty of space within, with rooms either side of a tiny central bar where the Kelham Island beers have pride of place, flanked by some microbrewery rivals – and Timmy Taylor's Landlord, when I called in. Bright golden **Best Bitter** (3.8%) has some soft marzipan notes, there is some orange and biscuit to the amber **Riders On The Storm** (4.5%) while the sweet, big tasting and faintly popcorn-accented favourite **Pale Rider** (5.2%) has been in the roster since the early days. Edward Wickett is carrying on the good work of his father, who died in 2012; brewery tours pull in thirsty visitors, the opening of the Tap and Tankard in Cambridge Street gives Kelham Island a city centre showcase for their wares.

Kirkstall Brewery

100 Kirkstall Road, Leeds, LS3 1HJ; T: 0113 898 0280;
E: info@verticaldrinks.com; W: www.kirkstallbrewerycompany.com

Few places can claim so long a history of brewing as Kirkstall. The Cistercian monks of Kirkstall Abbey started making beer here over 800 years ago and perhaps still would be, had it not been for the disastrous intervention of a King hell-bent on a split with Rome.

Some 300 years after the dissolution, the tradition was revived by the original Kirkstall Brewery which unloaded their barrels directly onto barges on the Leeds-Liverpool canal, which passed right behind the brewhouse and gave Kirkstall a ready means of transport to Lancashire and beyond.

For 150 years, they were a big player on the local scene, before they were closed down by giant owners Whitbread in 1983. The original stone-built tower brewery, complete with its chimney, is now home to up to 1,000 students, many of whom will no doubt have made acquaintance with beers from the new brewery which opened nearby in 2011, relocating to much larger premises in a former dairy in Kirkstall Road in 2016. Fragrant, hoppy **Kirkstall Pale** (4%) has become one of the ubiquitous beers on Leeds city centre bars; the excellent Brunswick being one of many which have given it a permanent place. The more potent **Three Swords** (4.5%) and full-bodied **Black Band Porter** (5.5%) are others worth seeking out. The former is a clean-tasting pale ale with some suggestions of lemon and lime, the latter a smooth and big-bodied red black ale with a hearty fireside blend of milky coffee and dark fruits.

As we go to press, work is continuing on a new on-site pub at the brewery, though the Old Bridge in Kirkstall, a serial winner of Leeds CAMRA's pub of the year prize, is the perfect place to make modern-day acquaintance with a brewing history that stretches back to the dark ages.

🍺 Dissolution Extra IPA (6%)

One of the very best beers I've tried during the long watches of this book's development, it takes its name from Henry VIII's ruinous sacking of the established church, which reduced majestic Kirkstall Abbey to a peaceful, grass-covered stone shell set in the heart of a public park.

This perfect pale, softly carbonated and deeply bitter India Pale Ale, is inspired by an IPA which was produced for export by the original Kirkstall brewery in Victorian times.

Though brewed to a strapping 6% it remains dangerously easy-drinking all the same; after a peachy aroma it packs in lots of piney, grassy hops, a real blast of thick-cut Oxford marmalade and a proper bitter finish. This is one of several Kirkstall ales available in can or bottle, a slightly less strong version is also available on draught.

Landlord's Friend Beers

Kershaw House Inn, Luddenden Lane, Halifax, HX2 6NW;
T: 01422 882222;

Brewed in quite small batches, each of the Landlord's Friend beers are sold in the pubs of Halifax and the Pennine hinterlands. They include warming and malty **Mr Cuddle** (4%), nutty amber ale **Mr Webster's** (4.2%) and fruity, chocolatey **Wilf** (4.1%).

Leeds Brewery

3 Sydenham Rd, Leeds, LS11 9RU; T: 0113 244 5866;
E: info@leedsbrewery.co.uk; W: www.leedsbrewery.co.uk

Big isn't always beautiful, but one can hardly blame
Leeds Brewery for shouting about its size. Once
small fry in a market monopolized by Tetley's, in a
mere decade Leeds has by happy accidents of timing
and nomenclature, become the city's new giant – a
fact celebrated on their home page and labels.

Just as Tetley's monocled huntsman was once a
fixture on the city's bars, now it seems most self-
respecting real ale pubs across the city serve the
crisp and refreshing **Leeds Pale** (3.8%). Full bodied
dark ale **Midnight Bell** (4.8%), massively-hopped
Hellfire (5.2%) and keg beers such as fruit-forward
IPA **Monsoon** (4.1%) and smoky, chocolatey stout **Gathering
Storm** (4.4%) add further dimensions to this modern local legend.

Leeds also followed Tetley's into the pub game, opening a string of
highly regarded pubs including the Midnight Bell in Holbeck and a
Brewery Tap close to city station. Though the chain has now passed
into the ownership of northern giants Cameron's, Leeds Brewery
beers remain a staple on the bars.

🍺 Leeds Best (4.3%)

This golden pale ale is a tad stronger than
the bitter of Joshua Tetley fame and the
brewer uses that extra legroom to pack in
some creamy caramel and significant
maltiness, all classically balanced by the
juicy bitterness of First Gold and Goldings
hops. Neither side out-muscles the other,
creating a beer both full-bodied and easy
drinking. And it's in that balance that
perhaps lies the brewery's success. While
some others have stretched the envelope
to create beers of great strength or
bewildering bitterness, this brewery's
straightforward, easy-going, mainstream
ales can always be relied on to deliver.

Legitimate Industries

10 Weaver Street, Leeds, LS4 2AU; W: www.legitimateworldwide.com

Based around the concept of a rapacious multi-national, Legitimate Industries' marketing strategy has given us beers with names like **Timeshare Scam** and **Double Agent**; as at Baytown (p18) and Fuggle Bunny (p68) the invention feeds into everything they do. Their website features a rogues' gallery of company directors and tells how the brewkit was asset stripped from a rival. The merchandise includes session IPA **Election Fraud** (4%) which has some legitimate mango and orange. The crisp, surprisingly floral **Tax Evasion** (4.4%) is probably as good a pilsner as Leeds has ever produced.

Linfit Brewery

Sair Inn, 139 Lane Top, Linthwaite, Huddersfield HD7 5SG; T: 01484 842370

Brewer Ron Crabtree was a legend in his own lifetime, which sadly ended in October 2016, when he died of throat cancer aged 79. For more than 30 years, his two-and-a-half barrel plant had produced a number of quality cask ales for sale at the Sair. Now brewer Ian Bagshaw has stepped into the breach, reviving ten of Ron's old recipes, including the full-bodied oaty stout **English Guineas** (4.7%) and the wittily named dark beer **Janet St Porter** (4.2%).

Little Brew

15-16 Auster Road, York, YO30 4XA; E: stu@littlebrew.co.uk

Having established his brewery in Camden in 2012, Stu Small relocated 200 miles up the East Coast Mainline to York in 2014. So far I've only managed to find his **Porter** (5%) but as a yardstick for the others, this is a big fruitcakey, malty, plummy, roasty, chocolatey triumph.

Little Critters Brewery

Unit 5, Neepsend Industrial Estate, 80 Parkwood Rd, Sheffield, S3 8AG;
T: 0114 276 3171; E: info@littlecrittersbrewery.com;
W: www.littlecrittersbrewery.com

The core list of this newcomer includes a flock of animal-themed ales including the pale **Golden Goose** (3.8%), oatmeal stout **Sleepy Badger** (4.5%), traditional English-style IPA **Malty Python** (4.8%) and the **Chameleon** series of single-hopped ales (5.5%).

📷 The Doctor's Orders
Glossop Road, Sheffield

The Doctor's Orders, close to Sheffield University campus, was voted Britain's best student pub in 2016, a move surely symbolic of a sea-change in young people's drinking tastes, given that this is Little Critters' brewery tap. At a time when students have embraced Britain's resurgent beer culture like never before, gained an enthusiasm for new flavours and taste experiences – and prized beers' local provenance – a student pub with its own brewery was always bound to be a winner.

It's an impressive building, occupying a prime spot above a main junction between Sheffield Children's Hospital, the Royal Hallamshire Hospital and the main university campus. It was previously a hotel, and its high-ceilinged lobby is now a broad open drinking area with comfortable leather sofas – and a long bar topped with ales from Little Critters' menagerie. Student medics get a healthy discount too.

Little Valley Brewery

Turkey Lodge, New Road, Hebden Bridge HX7 5TT; T: 01422 883 888;
E: info@littlevalleybrewery.co.uk; W: www.littlevalleybrewery.co.uk

Beer-loving Dutchman Wim van der Spek met partner Sue Cooper while they were both cycling in Nepal – he was going one way and she was going the other. After synchronising directions, the couple moved to Yorkshire in 2005 and established Little Valley Brewery high above Hebden Bridge. Here their devotion to great ale and concern for the planet go hand-in-hand with producing

some of the county's most interesting beers, which between them have garnered an impressive collection of awards.

Several honour Pennine placenames. There's moderately flowery and marmaladey **Cragg Vale Bitter** (4.2%), spicy, pithy, hazy **Hebden's Wheat** (4.5%) – twice a silver medal winner at the Great British Beer Festival – and the wonderfully rich and creamy **Stoodley Stout** (4.8%) all plums, coffee and chocolate. Straw-coloured and floral flagship ale **Withens Pale** (3.9%) takes its name from Top Withens, the windswept fell which reputedly inspired Emily Bronte, though its agreeable nature is perhaps more Cathy than Heathcliff.

There's a suggestion of white wine to the understated aroma of the anaemically-pale **Stage Winner** (3.5%) which has so exuberant a white head it might easily be mistaken for a specialist

Belgian lager. It celebrates the life of Yorkshire cyclist Brian Robinson – the first Brit ever to win a Tour de France stage. The old-school, well hopped and slightly grassy IPA **Python** (6%) was drunk by Palin, Cleese et al, during their reunion gigs in 2014.

Many of the Little Valley ales are available in bottle, others are sold through organic and vegan wholesaler Suma – and their first keg beers are coming soon.

🍺 LVBX (10%)

Stylishly packaged in a black presentation box and with a label tooled in expensive shiny gold script, LVBX clearly comes from the high end of the market. The label makes great play of this as a bottle conditioned, handcrafted organic barley wine, packed with "eight superior hops and malts".

Prising off the cap releases peaty and malty aromas; pouring it reveals its deep red-brown colour. If you hadn't read the label you might easily imagine this a sessionable brown ale or a mid-strength ruby porter. But those illusions are blown away when LVBX hits the palate and its whisky-like characteristics persist in a complex blend of woodsmoke and the sweetness of damsons which rather put me in mind of a Rusty Nail, that potent combination of Drambuie and scotch.

There are toasty caramel notes in there, but the iron-like firmness and sheer strength of this beer ensures that it quickly begins to work a soporific alchemy on the senses, its powerful influence remaining into a long liqueur coffee aftertaste.

Lords Brewing

Unit 15, Heath House Mill, Golcar, Huddersfield, HD7 4JW;
T: 07976 974162; W: www.lordsbrewing.com

Golcar Brewery owner John Broadbent inspired three brothers to establish Lords to set up in 2015, initially using his spare capacity but now using kit of their own. Beers include traditional Yorkshire bitter **Tithe House** (3.9%) with its characteristic balance of rich malt and amiably bitter English hops. By contrast, it is the strident citric, piney influence of American hops which dominate west coast pale ale **Helix** (5%), while there are some interesting spicy notes to **Havelock IPA** (5.9%).

Lost Industry Brewing

14a Nutwood Trading Estate, Limestone Cottage Lane, Sheffield, S6 1NJ;
T: 01142 316393;
E: beer@lostindustrybrewing.com;
W: www.lostindustrybrewing.com

Though only two years old, this family-run brewery's industrious attitude has already forged a reputation for their interesting and progressive expressions of both traditional and contemporary beers. Not having a regular brew has freed them to venture into wheat beers, sours, saisons, Belgian pales and dark ales – as well as the more familiar South Yorkshire territories of bitters, stouts, porters and pales. Boss Lesley Seaton tells me: "We're all beer geeks and we enjoy pushing the boundaries."

The only one I've caught up with so far is **Columbus** (6.8%) which is a hazy golden and slightly oily beer of such delicate, gentle nature you would never believe it to be so strong. There's orange and pineapple in the aroma and there are some nice tropical fruit notes in the taste and some spicy bitterness in the finish.

Magic Rock Brewing

Willow Park Business Centre, Willow Lane, Huddersfield HD1 5EB;
T: 01484 649823; E: sales@magicrockbrewing.com;
W: www.magicrockbrewing.com

Magic Rock is among that very special brand of brewers who have transcended humble, locally-based beginnings to become a nationwide craft sensation. Though founded as recently as 2011, production has now expanded to a sizeable 150-barrel plant, and the workforce to an impressive 30, including those charged with manning the pumps in the onsite taproom.

It fuses the enthusiasm of founder Richard Burhouse to the extraordinary brewing skills of Kelham Island alumnus Stuart Ross. The name references the Burhouse family gemstone business, and lends itself to an assortment of beers with a big top, freak show theme. They start with the pale floral sessionable **Ringmaster** (3.9%) whose moderate strength belies a beer of substance and significant fruit flavour – lemon, mango and lime are all in there. The amber **Rapture** (4.6%) supplies more of the same, but with more significant caramel notes, **Dark Arts** (6%) is an assertive gloopy, chocolatey, smoky stout with just a suggestion of dandelion and burdock, and there is a host of different brews under the **High Wire** name.

Though stronger than many, **Cannonball** (7.4%) is absolutely exemplary of the wonderful resurgence of India Pale Ale; its blend of resinous hops delivers a firm and complex taste, with apricot, grapefruit, peach, passion fruit and pine. Stronger still, **Bearded Lady** (10.5%) starts with a whiff of chocolate orange then layers the palate with an eiderdown of luxury vanilla and chocolate softness.

The tart, slightly sour, German-styled gose **Salty Kiss** (4.1%) was a gold medal winner in the fruit wheat beer section of the World Beer Cup. In the honey beer section, they picked up a silver prize for **Rhubarbarella** (7.2%), which is a braggot – a rarely visited blend of beer and mead, and a staple of Medieval Europe. Seasonals, specials and occasionals deliver yet more of the magic; distinctive pumpclips, cans and labels make them instantly recognisable on any bar.

Mallinsons Brewing Co

Unit 1 Waterhouse Mill, 65-71, Lockwood Road, Huddersfield, HD1 3QU;
T: 01484 654301; E: info@drinkmallinsons.co.uk;
W: www.drinkmallinsons.co.uk

Huddersfield favourites Mallinson's have been going almost a decade now, but stepped up production with a move to a new 15-barrel plant in 2012.

Rather than having permanent beers, Mallinson's produces a rolling core range which usually includes a couple of session-strength single hop ales in cask and a number of key kegs.

They took Beer of the Festival five times in a row at Huddersfield's Oktoberfest and can usually be found in some of the town's best beer houses – including their own taphouse the Corner – but they're widely distributed across the north.

It's worth seeking out the hazy golden **Motueka** (4%), whose name honours the hop variety which lends citric aroma to a significant beer of only moderate strength.

Mill Valley Brewery

Unit 5, Woodroyd Mills, South Parade, Cleckheaton, BD19 3AF;
T: 0113 815 1624;
E: info@millvalleybrewery.co.uk;
W: www.millvalleybrewery.co.uk

A new on-site bar is drawing in drinkers to this six-barrel brewery, where production is concentrated on three moderate-strength ales: the benign and gently hoppy **Luddite** (3.8%), the smooth and malty, toffee-accented **Mill Bitter** (4.3%) and the zingy, refreshing citric and hoppy **Mill Blonde** (4.2%) whose colour and character is derived from the Belgian pilsner malt in the brew.

A Huddersfield pub crawl

The town's railway station is a decent starting point for a circular crawl, not least because the excellent, column-fronted **Head of Steam** just outside is an example of how this chain continues to do well, now under the ownership of Cameron's.

From here you cross busy Castlegate to find the famous **Grove**, with its innumerable real ale lines, before negotiating the traffic to reach Rat Brewery's **Rat and Ratchet** in Chapel Hill (see p136). Cross back into the town centre to find pizzas, locally-brewed real ale and Moroccan styling at **Bar Maroc** in New Street, before moving on to the **Northern Taps** in Kingsgate and Mallinson's own **Corner,** nearby in Market Walk. From here, head due north for the quirky live music **Craft Beer House** in Wood Street and craft ale and gin joint **Arcade Beers** in Station Street.

Complete your trek with a visit to the well-preserved inter-war **Sportsman** in St John's Road, before a short walk back to the station and the **King's Head** where a recent refit revealed a fine ceiling and tiled floor.

South west of the town, the choice of ales at the **Shoulder of Mutton** in Lockwood and **Star** in Albert Street makes each well worth a visit; just north of it, a host of pleasures await at the **Magic Rock Tap** on the Willow Park Business Centre (see p109).

Further afield, the **Royal and Ancient** in Dalton Bank Road, **Little Bridge** in Slaithwaite, **Punch Tapas** in Honley, **Wine Bank** and **Railway** in Marsden and **Lower Royal George** in Scammonden are each doing their bit in the glorious cause of Yorkshire beer.

Milltown Brewing Co

The Old Railway Goods Yard, Scar Lane, Milnsbridge, Huddersfield HD3 4PE; T: 07946 589645; E: contact@milltownbrewing.co.uk; W: www.milltownbrewing.co.uk

Before this was a brewery, even before it was a railway goods yard, these premises were stables for delivery horses. The four-barrel plant was established here in 2011 and the beers regularly feature in Huddersfield pubs and those inside a 15-mile radius. **Sorachi Pale** (3.8%) gains its dazzling citrus character from Japanese hops, while **Willetts Notion** (3.9%) is a sessionable pale – but my favourite is the dark ruby ale **Maltissimo** (5.3%) whose firm malty and vanilla character is balanced by its dry bitter finish. The Dusty Miller at Longwood is the brewery tap.

Mithril Ales

Aldbrough St John, Richmond, DL11 7TL; T: 01325 374817 & 07889 167128; W: www.mithrilales.blogspot.co.uk; E: mithril58@btinternet.com

There are three regular ales here, the light and easy drinking **A66** (4%), malt-led amber beer **Dere Street** (3.8%) and my own favourite, the distinctively floral **Flower Power** (4.3%). But brewer Pete Fenwick creates a new beer every week – see his blog for the latest – and distributes them within 25 miles of the brewery. Mithril has won top prize at Darlington Beer Festival five times and four times at Richmond. Pubs in the very north of the county, like the Stanwick at Aldbrough St John and the White Swan at Gilling West are the best places to seek out Pete's handiwork.

Morton Collins Brewing

The Star Inn, 42 Standbridge Lane, Wakefield WF2 7DY; T: 01924 253659; E: gedmorton@aol.com

After being limited to appearances at local beer festivals, taking over at the Star has given Ged Collins a permanent outlet for his microbrewery. Beers include amiable, berry-ish **Wintersett Gold** (4.1%), full-flavoured stout **Stanley's Delight** (4.8%) and malty, earthy, biscuity **Strong Brown Ale** (4.7%).

Mitchells Hop House

352-354 Meadowhead, Sheffield, S8 7UJ; T: 0114 274 0311;
E: frankie@mitchellswine.co.uk; W: www.mitchellswine.co.uk

When the neighbouring Italian restaurant closed in 2016, long-established wine, beer and cigar store Mitchells decided to expand both their premises and their portfolio – pressing two old yoghurt churners into a new life as fermenters at the Mitchells Hop House Brewery. They include the floral and spice pale ale **Dennis** (4.5%), named after the company's founder; hearty, earthy 'beer and beef' bitter **Butchers** (4%) and the exuberant, zesty and refreshing **Marilyn** (4.3%), named after the rather kitsch statue of Marilyn Monroe which stands outside. Well-established pub and restaurant contacts offer a straightforward route to the on-trade while their own-brew competes for attention against 400 other bottled beers on Mitchells shelves.

Naylor's Brewery

Units 9-10 Midland Mills, Crosshills, BD20 7DT;
T: 01535 637451;
E: info@naylorsbrewery.co.uk;
W: www.naylorsbrewery.co.uk

Brothers Stephen and Robert established their
eponymous brewery in 2005; in a little over a
decade since they have established a reputation
for their traditional Yorkshire ales, particularly in
the west of Yorkshire and in the Dales. And the
Houses of Parliament too, where their golden
Cratchit's Cracker (4.2%) was the Christmas
beer of choice in 2016. Regular beers include
the zesty, zingy citric **Blonde** (4.3%) and the
dark amber, fruity **Old Ale** (5.9%); **Naylor's
Bitter** (3.8%) is a gently bitter, refreshing amber
ale – and I can vouch for its efficacy as a
counterpoint to a chicken Madras. Naylor's
produce three seasonal beers a month, while a
stunning list of bottled beers, including the
phenomenal liqueur-laced **Rum Baa Baa**
(6.2%), have eased them into the craft market.

🍺 Naylor's Ginger Beer (4.4%)

I know at least one reformed drinker who only
sups ginger beer these days. His local landlord
stocks his favourite brand specially, so he can
still be a regular without ever falling off the
wagon. Mind you, Naylor's Ginger Beer is
enough to send any anonymous addict back on
the binge. Its ginger is less pronounced than in
its alcohol-free counterparts, adding a tingle to
the nose and a little spicy zest to the palate. But
by every other measure it's a crafted English ale
pure and simple, refreshingly sharp, with fruit
and hops dominating a taste that gathers
momentum into a soothing, long-lasting
aftertaste.

Skipton's pubs

The centre of Skipton offers some interesting places to drink, though they're not always easy to find. **The Narrow Boat**, tucked away down a cobbled street beside the canal basin is an unspoiled drinking palace, now run by Market Town Taverns; while an airless alleyway leads to the excellent **Beer Engine** micropub. Around the corner in Swadford Street is the **Sound Bar** which offers an on-trend blend of great beer and vinyl records.

Of the pubs in the main street, I'd have to suggest the **Woolly Sheep**, where the narrow frontage belies a substantial pub which stretches back through to main drinking areas, a dining room, an attractive enclosed rear courtyard and to a number of outbuildings now beautifully restored as high-quality letting bedrooms. The bar offers the whole splendid Timothy Taylor roster.

A couple of miles south of Skipton is Cross Hills where two pubs renowned for good food are well worth a visit. The **Old White Bear** is a squat, stone fronted gem; while the **Beer Belly Kitchen** is an upstairs extension of Naylor's Brewery Tap. **Gallagher's Alehouse** in East Keltus is a second outpost for the Beer Engine.

Continuing south to Keighley, you find lots more Taylors in the pubs of their home town. The **Boltmakers Arms** in East Parade is the pub which gave its name to the brewery's sessionable former Champion Beer of Britain, while the community-oriented **Brown Cow** and stylish foody **Lord Rodney** both further the cause of the local brew.

Neepsend Brew Co

Unit 1-3 Lion Works, Mowbray Street, Sheffield, S3 8EN;
T: 0114 276 3406; E: gavin@neepsendbrewco.com

Though only established in 2015, Neepsend fought off a wealth of competition to be named Champion Beer of Sheffield in 2016, with their chocolatey, coffee-ish stout **Rollabout** (4.5%), which was brewed with the Sheffield Steel Rollergirls team. Their only regular beer is the straightforward, moderately-hopped **Blonde** (4%), while they also produce seasonal and special ales including hazy, slightly grassy **Mandarin** (4.3%), New Zealand pale ale **Sharpshooter** (4.7%) which is hopped with Nelson Sauvin and Pacific Jade, and American pale ale **Osiris** (4.2%), 2016 champion at Stockport beer festival.

Nomadic Beers

29 Skelton Terrace, LS9 9ES;
T: 07868 345228;
E: nomadicbeers@gmail.com;
W: www.nomadicbeers.co.uk

Funky merchandise, a tap takeover of a steam railway, a distinctive green delivery van and an all-female brewing day – though only established in 2017, Katie Marriott's Nomadic Brewery is already doing things a little differently. Operating from the Burley Street Brewhouse (see p45), Katie has decided against a core range, though three of her rotating recipes have already proved popular enough to brew again. These are the **Bitter** (4.3%), a great balance of malty biscuit with fruity hops; her big aromatic **IPA** (6.1%) and – Katie's own favourite – the smooth and silky **Oatmeal Pale** (4.9%).

Nine Standards

– See Settle

The Nook Brewhouse

Victoria Square, Holmfirth, HD9 2DN; T: 01484 682373;
E: office@thenookbrewhouse.co.uk; W: www.thenookbrewhouse.co.uk

In 2009 a local brewing tradition was revived with the opening of a brewhouse behind The Nook pub where an ancient brewery once stood. Documents and deeds on display in the pub highlight the history of the site and a proud brewing heritage which dates back to 1754. Regular ales include sessionable, mid-brown – and not especially bitter – **Yorks Bitter** (3.7%), sharp and citric **Baby Blond** (3.8%), golden and floral **Best** (4.2%) and the full-bodied, slightly treacly **Oat Stout** (5.2%). The list is completed with a good selection of occasional ales and many of them are available in bottle, labels adorned with the grotesque cartoons of the Nook pumpclips.

🏷 The Nook

This splendid old pub is the ideal place to try the beers brewed out back. Its Sunday name is the Rose and Crown, but this 250-year-old stone built alehouse, squeezed between a claustrophobic alleyway and the River Ribble, has been called the Nook for longer than most people can remember.

Live music nights, real ale, a beer garden and its tourist-trap spot in the heart of the Summer Wine village, offer something for everyone. Walkers, CAMRA members, those drawn to concerts at the lovely old Picturedrome opposite – even the coach parties searching for Nora's house and Ivy's Cafe – all make their way to this curiously-shaped pub, an untidy knot of irregular rooms clustered around a tiny central bar.

Siblings Ian Roberts and Sheila Sutton took the reins here in 2000 following the untimely death of their father, David Roberts, landlord here for almost 30 years. They have continued his work, maintaining the pub's proud place in the Good Beer Guide, while expanding the business with the brewhouse, a new tap house, and bed and breakfast accommodation.

During the town's jazz festival, the Nook is in position-A, hosting gigs and serving locally-brewed ale to all comers. The addition of a film festival to the local calendar has given the Nook further opportunity to get in on the act.

North Brewing

Unit 6, Taverners Walk Industrial Estate, Sheepscar Grove, Leeds LS7 1AH;
T: 0113 345 3290; E: sales@northbrewing.com;
W: www.northbrewing.com

North Bar Group has been a driving force behind the craft beer movement in Leeds. From its modest beginnings in Briggate, the group has built organically, its expansion into new premises, keeping roughly in pace with its growing reputation for quality beer, knowledgeable staff and laid-back atmosphere. It was perhaps only a matter of time before North was further seized by the spirit of the times to open its own brewery.

"I'm completely self-taught," brewer Sebastian Brink tells me over a beer at the bar. "I started off in home brewing." He widened his experience at the city's Golden Owl microbrewery (p71), before joining North Bar, where he has been given the freedom to experiment with some novel recipes. And while I'm more than happy to hold our conversation over a pint of refreshing session beer **Prototype** (3.8%) or his traditional nutty caramel **Bulkhead Brown** (4.5%), Seb is keen to show off the more esoteric end of the spectrum.

The unappetisingly-named **Bog Myrtle** (5.5%) is named after a scrubby Scots plant known since Viking times for its remarkable properties as a pick-me-up and an insect repellent. It predates the use of hops – and here Seb uses it as an alternative to the piney, citric characteristics of Simcoe. The toasted coconut porter **Full Fathom Five** (6.5%) and the Belgian-styled **Bret** (4.7%), made with wild yeast brettanomyces, extend further opportunities to stretch his legs as a brewer.

Norland Beers

4c Ladyship Business Park, Mill Lane, Halifax; T: 07475 085385;
E: norlandbeersltd@outlook.com

Thirst quenching, quaffable bitter **Barnstormers** (3.8%) is the best known product from a brewer which began life at Bridestones, and has since re-located to premises first used by Oates and now by Felix, an off-shoot of Junction. Brewing sometimes seems a complicated, incestuous world.

 Transmission (6.9%)

Though there are some soft, fruity aromatic notes to this pale amber West Coast IPA, it's only when it hits the palate that it really starts throwing its weight around. Its strength manifests itself in an immediate blast of the rich, big-tasting hops and its full-on bitterness develops into a complex cocktail of grapefruit and passion fruit, almost as though the brew has been spiked with a syrupy concentrate. And, curiously for an IPA – whose roots lie in the need for a cooling, refreshing, revitalising beer for the troops of the Indian Raj – its formidable potency lends some surprising warming qualities.

North Riding Brewery

Unit 9, Betton Business Park, Racecourse Road, East Ayton, Scarborough, YO13 9HD; T: 01723 864845; E: adrian@northridingbrewery.com; W: www.northridingbrewery.com

American hops seem to be key to the recipes at this new kid on the block, with their fruity pale ales **Cascade** (4%), **Citra** (4.5%) and **Mosaic** (4.3%) each named after big-selling varieties. Interestingly, their **US Session IPA** (3.8%) is brewed once monthly with three different US hops in each time. Aussie and New Zealand hops feature in some of their seasonals. The North Riding Brewpub in North Marine Road offers a home to these beers – and plenty more.

North Union Brewing Co

Arch 25, Sussex St, Sheffield, S4 7YY; T: 01909 519891 / 07962 067747; E: info@northunionbrewing.co.uk; W: www.northunionbrewing.co.uk

A railway arch in the centre of Sheffield is home to a brewery which only opened in 2015 but is already talking about creating a taproom on site and conducting brewery tours. The five hop varieties which go into **North Union Pale Ale** (5.5%) between them summon a significant burst of grapefruit, mango and passion fruit, the refreshing **Amber Lager** (4.6%) is a perfect barbecue beer, while the wonderful deep brown Abbey-style **Dubbel** (6.5%) is a full-on, toasty, malty, chocolatey, Christmas cake assault on the senses.

North Yorkshire Brewing

Pinchinthorpe Hall, Guisborough, TS14 8HG; T: 01287 630200; E: sales@nybrewery.co.uk;

Yorkshire's most northerly brewery uses its own spring water to create cask and bottle-conditioned ales noted for their malty, yeasty characteristics. **Best** (3.6%) is a simple session beer, **Cereal Killer** (4.5%) a light and fruity wheat beer, while full-bodied and vanilla-accented brown ale **Boro Best** (4%) keeps the Riverside faithful from having to drink Newky Brown. **Archbishop Lee's Ruby Ale** (4%) honours the churchman who had the unenviable task of replacing the unfortunate Wolsey as Archbishop of York. The beer looks gorgeous, a nice enticing copper brown topped by a firm ivory head, with a gentle yeasty aroma. Malt is the dominant taste though some surprising bitterness breaks through in a strong finish.

Northallerton Brewery

2 Binks Close, Standard Way Business Park, Northallerton, DL6 2YB;
T: 01609 258226; W: www.northallertonbrewery.co.uk

The closure of much-loved Wall's County Town Brewery in April 2016 left a sizeable hole in the lives of drinkers across the north of the county. A number of community shareholders came together to found this new company which has filled that gap and revived David Wall's popular recipes. There are more than 20 owners: "It's landlords, CAMRA members, the local public, even relatives of people who work here," says brewery manager Grace Aird.

Brewer Mark Hutchinson

This groundswell of enthusiasm managed to breathe new life into the plant, which sits just a stone's throw from the East Coast Mainline, towards the end of 2016. "We just missed out on the Christmas trade, unfortunately!"

Buying the recipes enabled Northallerton to put Wall's big-selling and quite markedly hop-heavy bitter **Gun Dog** (3.8%) back onto the region's bars. Others to be revived include mild and emollient pale ale **Snow Storm** (3.8%), chocolate-orangey **Northallerton Dark** (4.4%) and big, breezy, citric and golden IPA **Trail Runner** (5.2%).

"We're all about cask ale, sold within 35 miles of here," says Grace, but adds that brewer Mark Hutchinson is keen to extend his repertoire. Even so, they are cautious about expanding their product list too far beyond the tried and tested beers: "Drinkers around here are quite traditional, quite conservative," says Mark. "I'd love to do a wheat beer, but there's still the perception here that if it's hazy, it's off." So his first new product keeps the brewery on safe ground: the stout **Lizzie D** (4.4%) derives coffee undertones and blackcurrant notes from roasted malt and Bramling Cross hops in the brew.

Though many pubs in Northallerton itself are tied to other breweries, the free trade in surrounding villages is a rich trading ground for the new owners.

THE OLD FLAX STORE

NORTHERN MONK
BREW CO

NORTHERN MONK
BREW CO

OPENING TIMES
MONDAY: CLOSED
TUESDAY: 11am – 11pm
WEDNESDAY: 11am – 11pm
THURSDAY: 11am – 11pm
FRIDAY: 10am – 12am
SATURDAY: 10am – 1am
SUNDAY: 10am – 8pm

124

Northern Monk Brew Co

The Old Flax Store, Marshalls Mill, Holbeck, Leeds, LS11 9YJ;
T: 0113 243 6430; E: drink@northernmonkbrewco.com;
W: www.northernmonkbrewco.com

Before establishing its own brewery in a Grade II listed building in Leeds' industrial revolution heartland of Holbeck, 2014, Northern Monk began as a gypsy brewery, nomadically brewing in other breweries' premises by contract. The brewery is in the ground floor of Marshall's former flax mill, upstairs is a taproom and kitchen and above that a versatile event space.

In this short time, Northern Monk's reputation for innovative, quality craft ales has grown so rapidly that they are already expanding brewing to a second site while their new Refectory Brew Company brand will showcase the skills and passion of their staff. Lashings of American hops typify the Northern Monk approach, as in the Simcoe and Mosaic hops blended to toasty, hearty, fruity good effect in **Dark Arches** (6.7%). **Bombay Dazzler** (4.8%) is an Indian spiced witbier, tangerine-dominated session IPA **Eternal** (4.1%) was a medal winner at the prestigious World Beer Cup in 2016 while **True North** (3.7%) is a classic Yorkshire pale.

🍺 Northern Star (5.9%)

By the time the Campaign for Real Ale was founded in 1971, the porter brewing style, once a refreshing drink of choice for the working man, was all but extinct. The overwhelming success of the Campaign has given brewers the confidence to revive and expand the genre; the widespread availability of this new breed of porters has encouraged consumers to rediscover this most ancient of beer styles. This mocha porter is Northern Monk's take on the style – rich and strong, with ground coffee beans lending a luxurious richness which might come as a surprise to the London wharf and market porters who once made this style their very own. Northern Star is jet black, with a foaming head, suggestions of dark chocolate and hazelnut to the taste and some bitter smokiness in the finish.

Old Mill Brewery

Mill Street, Snaith, DN14 9HU;
T: 01405 861813;
E: sales@oldmillbrewery.co.uk;
W: www.oldmillbrewery.co.uk

Around 150 years ago, Snaith was well served by brewers and maltsters, though the emergence of the major breweries in nearby Tadcaster saw the trade die out.

Only with the opening of Old Mill Brewery in 1983 did this great craft return to a town whose origins lie before the Norman Conquest. Production is concentrated on a very traditional selection – a roasty dark **Mild** (3.4%), a nicely malty **Bitter** (3.9%), and a chocolatey **Yorkshire Porter** (4.4%) augmented by a list of monthly seasonal specials.

Though Old Mill beers can be found in a 30-mile radius of Snaith, the village's excellent Brewers Arms is very much the tap.

🍺 Blonde Bombshell (4%)

Pale barley malt, wheat and Czech hops go into producing this almost anaemic beer, one of Old Mill's permament cask and bottled ales. Once poured it has some suggestions of craft cider, with dry appley aromas before the spicy, clovey elements you might expect of a wheat beer take over on the palate. A little gentle malt emerges in the aftertaste of a beer which delivers at least some of the excitement you might expect a blonde bombshell to provide.

🏛 The Mission, Posterngate, Hull

Right in the heart of Hull's historic Old Town, these rather imposing premises opened in the 1920s as a Mission to Seamen, a Christian welfare charity which serves merchant crews around the world.

It has now been re-purposed as an alehouse offering the whole Old Mill range, hearty pub food – and by night it becomes a lively night-spot.

As someone whose family tradition is rooted in muscular non-conformism – and who rebelled against it, only to be seduced by a brilliant Leeds goth band of the same name – somewhere called The Mission is entirely irresistible.

Old Spot Brewery

Manor Farm, Station Road,
Cullingworth, Bradford, BD13 5HN;
T: 01535 275566;
W: www.oldspotbrewery.com

Old Spot began brewing in
2005, using kit salvaged from
the Boat brewery in Castleford.

The range includes the coffee
and liquorice accented dark mild
Darkside Pup (3.6%); simple,
slightly orangey chestnut bitter
Light But Dark (4%); full-
bodied, slightly grassy golden
ale **OSB** (4.5%) and substantial
sweetish porter **Spot O'Bother**
(5.5%).

On The Edge Brewery

Woodseats, Sheffield;
T: 07854 983197;
E: ontheedgebrew@gmail.com;
W: www.ontheedgebrew.com

Thomas Richards and Luisa
Golob operate a tiny brewing
plant in their kitchen. No brew is
the same as the last and the
beers go to pubs such as the
Beer House in Sheffield's
Ecclesall Road and the interesting
Mallard on Worksop station. A
string of awards from local
festivals – including a runner-up
prize in CAMRA's 2012 Beer of
Sheffield contest – underline the
quality from this most micro of
microbreweries.

Phil Garvey at the Cap and Collar.

A Bradford pub crawl

A little corner of Bradford has been transformed by the arrival of three wonderful beer bars. First there's the hipster **Sparrow** in North Parade, with its ever-changing choice of cask, keg and bottled beers just along from the wonderfully individual **Record Cafe** (see p25). Just around the corner is **Bradford Brewery Tap** in Westgate (see p32) from where it's a short walk to the much older **New Beehive**, where 1930s gas light fittings and a real fire help secure this traditional real ale inn a place on CAMRA's list of historic pub interiors.

In a maze of Victorian tunnels beneath the heart of the city, the new underground retail complex **Sunbridge Wells** offers a host of drinking opportunities, including craft beer bar **The Rose and Crown**.

Close by in Saltaire are the quirky **Fanny's Alehouse**, Ossett Brewery's **Hop** – and the splendid little micropub **Cap and Collar**, where several of the beers are served direct from casks racked up behind the bar. In nearby Shipley, the **Oddfellow** is another worth seeking out.

In Wibsey on the south-western fringes of the city, the **Hooper** micropub works to a very simple formula of great beer, great atmosphere – and no frills. Out-of-town breweries **Bingley** (p24) and **Saltaire** (p144) each have an on-site tap, while bars like the **Idle Cock**, **Idle Draper** and **Idle Working Mens Club** trade high on the curious name of the northern suburb.

Ossett Brewery

Low Mill Road, Ossett, WF5 8ND; T: 01924 237160;
E: brewery@ossett-brewery.co.uk;
W: www.ossett-brewery.co.uk

Almost 20 years of steady growth has seen Ossett build from a microbrewery into one of the region's major players with 23 pubs, nationwide distribution, and with three craft breweries – Rat, Fernandes and Riverhead – added to the fold.

The success is founded on four solidly performing real ales: gentle, malty **Yorkshire Blonde** (3.9%), deep ruby, fruity and spicy **Big Red** (4%), multi-award-winning crisp, dry and citric **Silver King** (4.3%) and premium pale ale **Excelsior** (5.2%).

Seasonal and limited edition ales extend the choice still further. Ossett's excellent chain of Hop pubs – there are branches in Wakefield, York and Saltaire – are the ideal place to immerse yourself in the whole Ossett experience. A visit to the Leeds branch, set into the brooding dark arches below city station, where water rushes beneath and trains rumble overhead, is a chance to marvel at the ingenuity of industrial revolution engineering.

Treacle Stout

The addition of rich dark treacle adds depth, substance and some real sweetness to Ossett's interpretation of this ancient brewing style. The label's teaspoon dripping glistening black gloop leaves you in no doubt what to expect.

And though its influence isn't so apparent on the nose, as soon as this beer crosses the threshold, the treacle asserts itself, lending a smooth lathering of warmth and sweetness across the palate. There are some nice vanilla notes in there too and a gentle, dusty dry finish, tempting you to open another.

Outlaw Brewery – see Rooster's.

Partners Brewery

589 Halifax Road, Hightown,
Liversedge, WF15 8HQ;
T: 01924 457772;
E: sales@partnersbrewery.co.uk;
W: www.partnersbrewery.co.uk

Mungo and shoddy were once products of the heavy woollen district, cloth made from recycling rags and scraps of material. Partners has recycled the dyehouse of the Henry Day Mungo and Shoddy Mill into a brewhouse and established a solid local reputation for ales like the crisp **Blonde** (3.9%), the not overly-hoppy but more mainstream **American Craft Ale** (4.5%) and – best of all – gloriously hoppy, fruity, wheat-beer influenced **Tabatha** (6%). The brewery recently absorbed Ossett's Bob's Brewery into their operation, bringing the light and flowery **White Lion** (4.3%) – and other colours of Lion – into the portfolio.

Pennine Brewing Co

Well Hall Farm, Bedale, DL8 2PX;
T: 01677 470111;
E: sales@pennine-brewing.co.uk;
W: www.pennine-brewing.co.uk

A dizzying, dazzling domain of specials and seasonals means that the Bedale brewery, which decamped from its first home in Batley in 2013, has always got something different to offer.

These augment a core roster: the mellow, creamy and easy-going **Best Bitter** (3.9%), hoppy, golden **Natural Gold** (4.2%), significantly fruity **Real Blonde** (4%), and the sparkling **Amber Necker** (3.8%).

Pennine's standout performer is the blonde and caramelly **Hair of the Dog** (3.9%) which has garnered a string of awards and is a "must-have" beer wherever you find it.

The Carpenters Arms

Vale of Mowbray pubs

It probably wasn't uppermost in His mind, but when the creator ordained that the sun would rise in the east and set in the west, he ensured that customers at the **Carpenters Arms** in Felixkirk would have the perfect backdrop for their evening pints, night after Yorkshire night. Picture windows and a raised wooden terrace allow drinkers to admire the sublime majesty that comes with a weeping sun falling beneath a rippling blanket of cloud over the Vale of Mowbray.

This stretch of low-lying land between the North York Moors and the Hambleton Hills to the east and the Yorkshire Dales to the west is dotted with villages, many of them home to traditional Yorkshire pubs, like the seriously foody **Buck Inn** at Maunby and the curiously named **Otterington Shorthorn** in Newby Wiske – try saying that when you're drunk. But there are plenty more.

In Thirsk is the **Little 3**, rich in character and with an 800-year history; in Northallerton, county town of North Yorkshire, are Market Town Taverns' **Tithe** and the CAMRA favourite **Tickle Toby**, which takes its curious name from an 18th century pickpocket. His continued ownership of the town's **Stumble Inn** has allowed David Wall to maintain a connection to the brewery which once bore his name. He serves Northallerton Brewery (p123) ales in his pub; his own pet still has pride of place on the Gun Dog pumpclip.

Just east of the town is the majestic **Cleveland Tontine**, from the same stable as the Carpenters, and with the same focus on quality dining. Bedale has a host of traditional inns – the **Three Coopers** and **Green Dragon** both merit a mention – but the newly-opened **Bridge Beer Cafe**, with its accent on Belgian ales, is a funky, atmospheric addition to the scene.

The Cleveland Tontine

Quirky Ales

Ash Lane, Garforth, Leeds, LS25 2HG; T: 0113 286 2072;
E: info@quirkyales.com; W: www.quirkyales.com

On an industrial estate on the edge of Garforth, hidden away behind low-rise workshops and warehouses, something remarkable is taking place. Led by a former police firearms commander, a new brewhouse and bar is drawing a regular following to this most unpromising of locations.

It's the brainchild of Mike Quirk who began home brewing after handing in his warrant card and looking for something less stressful to do with his time. So it might have stayed but for the timely intervention of investors John Fergusson and Andrew Milner who helped take the business from the quaint and quirky to the quite extraordinary.

Their support and encouragement allowed Mike to trade his tiny brew kit for some serious stainless steel and install it at this unprepossessing warehouse, just outside the centre of Garforth, where occasional guest brew days give all comers the chance to try their hand at making a beer.

The pocket handkerchief taproom next door has just a handful of tables, while other drinkers stand or lean on the bar, or admire the impressive line-up of bottled beers on sale. It's open from Thursday to Sunday, and it must have taken quite a leap of faith to believe that drinkers would come here, but they do. Mike even manages to shoehorn some live acts onto an impromptu stage beside the door, though accommodating anyone bigger than a duo wouldn't leave room for their equipment. Or an audience.

With his output limited by the size of the fermenting vessels in the brewhouse next door, Mike brews three times a week, and the choice on draught varies from day to day. They include softly-spoken grapefruity pale ale **Maxima** (4.1%), unassuming fruity **Blonde** (3.8%), malty, woodsmokey **Phoenix** (5.3%) and light, easy drinking **Porter** (3.5%) which makes for an unusual alternative dark session beer. The pick of the bunch for me is the impressively substantial, rich red brown **Classic** (5.7%), packed with the sweetness of dark fruit and bonfire toffee and undoubtedly a homage to Theakston's Old Peculier.

The Fleece at Pudsey and Gascoigne in the Barwick regularly take Quirky casks, while beer festival crowds from across the region have been quick to warm to Mike's ales, which are also available in bottle.

LTD

OM

05/16

Mike Quirk

Rat Brewery

40, Chapel Hill, Huddersfield, HD1 3EB; T: 01484 542400;
E: ratcrafted@rat-brewery.co.uk; W: www.rat-brewery.co.uk

The Rat and Ratchet was established as a brewpub in 1994, and though brewing ceased for several years it began again in 2011, following the pub's purchase by Ossett Brewery.

Brewer Paul Spencer describes himself as Head Rodent – and he clearly has a penchant for puns, with beers such as the uber-hopped IPA **Rat Against the Machine** (7%), **Imperial Stout Ratsputin** (7.4%) and bottled barley wine **Grapes Of Rat** (10%).

Regular products include pale and bitter **White Rat** (4%), dark coffee-ish porter **Black Rat** (4.5%) and the straw-coloured, wine-nosed, New Zealand-hopped **King Rat** (5%) – with beers available in cask and keg.

Regather Brewery

57-59 Club Garden Road, Sheffield, S11 8BU; T: 0114 273 1258;
E: info@regather.net; W: www.regather.net

The Regather Co-Operative is based in the historic Horn Handle Works in Sharrow, just south of Sheffield city centre.

Beyond the regular **Pale Ale** (4.8%) and **IPA** (5.3%), both of which are big favourites in the Regather bar, the 150-litre craft brewery produces interesting, well thought out, cosmopolitan-influenced bottled ales.

Achtzig Deutsche Mark Bitte (5.2%) is a dark, malty, Scottish 80-shilling brewed with German and Vienna malts; **Winter Solstice** (5.6%) is a crisp, dry, full-flavoured IPA given a sharp grapefruit finish by Mandarina Bavaria hops. **Edelreiss** (5.7%) is a complex German Weissbier, slightly darker than you would expect, with distinctive bubblegum and banana flavours; uber-hopped citrus-heavy **Sheffield Nevada** (5.6%) is a tribute to the classic Sierra Nevada pale.

Regather offers Brew Day experiences for customers to design a beer and help with the brewing process – an ideal Christmas or birthday present.

Revolutions Brewing

Unit B7, Whitwood Enterprise Park, Castleford, WF10 5PX;
T: 01977 552649; E: andrew@revolutionsbrewing.co.uk;
W: www.revolutionsbrewing.co.uk

Following the success of their rather malty Vienna-style lager **Severina** (5%) which was a SIBA national champion in 2016, the multi-award-winning Castleford brewer has been busy unveiling some new keg lagers, including toasty schwarzbier **Dominion** (5%) and helles-styled **Sanctuary** (5%). These have been added to a range which includes big-bodied London porter **Clash** (4.5%), the sessionable pale ale **Candidate** (3.9%) and the dark, fruity malty amber ale **Treasure** (4.5%). If it's not obvious already, all the beer names have rock and new wave connections.

Richmond Brewing Company

Units 1-2, The Old Station, Station Yard, Richmond, DL10 4LD;
T: 01748 828266; E: enquiries@richmondbrewing.co.uk;
W: www.richmondbrewing.co.uk

In 2016, new fermenting and conditioning tanks and a bar for visitors to sample the beers doubled the size of the brewery based in Richmond's stunning riverside Victorian railway station which is home to a number of artisan food producers. Their core products include the light and golden **Station Ale** (4%), the distinctly bitter mild **Swale** (3.7%) and the dark, malty, slightly sweet **Stump Cross** (4.7%) which is brewed with water from Stump Cross Caverns near Pateley Bridge. All three are also available in bottle.

Ridgeside Brewery

Unit 24, Penraevon 2 Industrial Estate,
Jackson Road, Leeds, LS7 2AW;
T: 07595 380568; E:
accounts@ridgesidebrewery.co.uk;
W: www.ridgesidebrewery.co.uk

The death of Simon Bolderson in 2014 robbed Leeds brewing of a legend. In just four years he had established Ridgeside's reputation for quality craft ales which were a guarantee of quality on bars around the city, not least at the excellent East of Arcadia nearby, which gave him a permanent place on the bar.

Thankfully new owners are ensuring the Ridgeside story continues. Tart blueberry and melon **Sourbet** (4.5%) reveals much about the new regime of head brewer Matt Lovatt and Colombian business partners Jorge Gonzalez Moore and Juan Mendoza. There's a willingness to innovate – this is the only Leeds brewery doing full-batch sours – while the Pythonesque label of a woman whose head has been sliced open to reveal a juicy melon inside shows designer Juan's avant garde leanings.

Equator (5.5%) is the epitome of a modern IPA, chock-full of grapefruit and passion fruit, the product of heavy Californian hopping late in the brew. **Roosevelt** (4.5%) is a simpler, more placid product of this same refreshing American influence. Their greatest tribute to Simon is that two of his characteristically traditional British beers – and rock-themed names – have been maintained: **Jailbreak** (4%) is an easy-going pale session ale, **Black Night** (5%) a fulsome sweetish oatmeal stout.

Riverhead Brewery

2 Peel Street, Marsden, Huddersfield, HD7 6BR;
T: 01924 237160;
E: brewery@ossett-brewery.co.uk; W: www.ossett-brewery.co.uk

Though now owned by regional heavyweight Ossett Brewery, Riverhead remains a tiny two-barrel plant whose production goes largely to the brewery tap above. Brewster Lisa Handforth has developed a catalogue of seasonal beers infused with locally-sourced fruits and herbs such as **Sherbert Lemon** (4.1%) and **Sour Cherry Red** (3.9%).

These are in addition to her reservoir-themed regular beers, the gentle, under-stated, lightly fruity **Butterley Bitter** (3.8%), the more assertively caramel and biscuitty **March Haigh** (4.6%) and the rich and full-bodied **Redbrook Premium** (5.5%).

Rooster's Brewing Co

Unit 3, Grimbald Park, Wetherby Road, Knaresborough, HG5 8LJ;
T: 01423 865959; E: hello@roosters.co.uk;
W: www.roosters.co.uk

Years from now, when someone traces the bloodline of the craft beer revolution, they will find Rooster's writ large in the DNA. It began life in 1993 in Harrogate, where brewer Sean Franklin embraced the new hop varieties emerging in America's Yakima Valley, and put them front centre in a series of elegant, crisp, juicy pale ales. It's not stretching a point too far to say that the sparkling spicy, floral, **Yankee** (4.3%) is a beer that turned the British brewing scene on its head, and though now relatively tame compared to some weightily-hopped newcomers, they owe much to its bravery and ultimately its success.

Sean retired in 2011, and worked alongside twins Oliver and Tom Fozard to ensure a smooth transition to the new owners. Though they have substantially expanded the range, and invested heavily in increasing capacity, their beers remain true to his legacy. They include the floral, slightly sweet, grassy **YPA** (4.1%), full-bodied, plummy coffee porter **Londinium** (5.5%) and the orange-accented entry-level pale ale **Buckeye** (3.5%).

Newly-introduced session IPA **Twenty Four Seven** (4.7%) derives complex fruit character from a cocktail of American Amarillo, Simcoe and Chinook hops – plus fashionable New Zealander Nelson Sauvin. The selection extends yet further through quarterly, monthly and limited edition specials.

🍺 Baby-Faced Assassin (6.1%)

Rooster's reputation as a trendsetter didn't end with their enthusiastic adoption of American hops. In 2015 the brewery installed a micro-canning plant in their Knaresborough Brewery and started putting some of their award-winning beers into cans, a move once derided by the purists. There's a really enticing tropical fruit blast to the aroma of golden Baby-Faced Assassin, one of the first three Rooster's beers given the aluminium treatment. This continues into a complex taste, heavy with mango and oranges, but so delightfully easy drinking that its gentle nature offers a false sense of security. Only when you read its strength in the small print do you realise the dangerous nature of this aptly-named assassin.

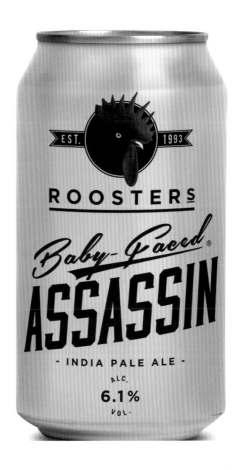

Rudgate Brewery

2 Centre Park, Marston Business Park, Tockwith, YO26 7QF;
T: 01423 358382; E: sales@rudgatebrewery.co.uk;
W: www.rudgatebrewery.co.uk

There's a whole heap of history here, from the Romans to the Roundheads to the RAF.

Marston Moor was the site of a pivotal civil war battle; 300 years later it was the wartime base for Halifax Bombers.

Established in 1992 in the airfield's former ammunition store, Rudgate is named after the old Roman road which crossed the Vale of York. Their entry-level product is the **Jorvik Blonde** (3.8%), an attractive golden beer of soft gingerish aroma and the kind of fruit and marzipan flavours which are usually associated with darker, stronger, winter warmers.

Ruby Mild (4.4%) has some delicious liquorice and toffee on the nose, then a big blast of soft fruits on the palate, followed by a surge of unexpected late bitterness.

Valkyrie (5%) is a nicely-constructed American pale ale, that's bursting with oranges and tangerines and is rather sweeter and more benign than its forbidding Wagnerian name suggests.

Blonde is available in keg, several are available in bottle – and three specials every month keep things interesting.

The famous old Spotted Ox in Tockwith is one of my favourite places to commune with the latest phase in this evolving history.

Ryedale Brewing

Hardings House, Hardings Lane, Cross Hills, Keighley, BD20 7AD;
T: 01535 637026; E: info@ryedalebrewing.co.uk;
W: www.ryedalebrewing.co.uk

Family issues persuaded David and Tony Williams to move their brewery from its original home near York to new premises at Keighley. And after concentrating on traditional cask ales, like the pale golden **Angler** (3.8%) and the quintessential dark Yorkshire bitter **Rambler** (3.8%), they now plan to edge toward the hoppy end of the market: "That seems to be the way everyone's going," says Tony. Though it was still in fermenting tanks when we spoke, he has high hopes for the significantly hopped **Harvester** (4%); Gallaghers Alehouse in Cross Hills is the ideal place to check on its success.

British Guild of Beer Writers

Renowned Yorkshire journalists Barrie Pepper and the late Michael Jackson were among founding fathers of a group set up in 1988 to improve the standards of writing on beer, brewing and pubs – and the Guild's growth has reflected that of the popularity of the product. Both Jackson and prolific Barnsley-born author Pete Brown are serial winners of its highest accolade, British Beer Writer of the Year. I won once, but this may have been an administrative error. **www.beerguild.co.uk**

Salamander Brewing

22 Harry Street, Bradford, BD4 9PH; T: 01274 652323;
E: info@salamanderbrewingcompany.co.uk;
W: www.salamanderbrewingcompany.co.uk

A former pork pie factory was given the brewery treatment in 1999 and its on-site bar is an ideal place to linger over a quality range. They include malty and gently-hopped **Blondie** (4%), Champion Beer at the city's 2015 beer festival; bittersweet copper-coloured **Mudpuppy** (4.2%) whose distinctive hop character is derived from Progress and East Kent Goldings hops; refreshing premium pale **Golden Salamander** (4.5%) and the intense **Bright Black Porter** (4.8%) with its luxurious rum and caramel overtones.

Saltaire Brewery

County Works, Dockfield Road, Shipley, Bradford, BD17 7AR;
T: 01274 594959; E: info@saltairebrewery.co.uk;
W: www.saltairebrewery.co.uk

Though technically in neighbouring Shipley, Saltaire Brewery has always been keen to play up its connections to the famous World Heritage Site village, whose model of enlightened capitalism made Sir Titus Salt a revered figure both for his workers and his fellow mill-owners. He built his fortune on cloth woven from the wool of the alpaca; the care he took for the welfare of his workforce was borne of fervent Christian belief.

Based in an old generating station which once supplied the electricity for Bradford's trams, Saltaire has really established itself as a powerhouse since brewing began a decade ago – with Salt's Mill livery an increasingly familiar sight on real ale handpulls, keg fonts and on the supermarket shelves. A significant expansion of the brewery is currently under way.

Very pale **Saltaire Blonde** (4%) has some interesting sweet malty characteristics which balance its significant hoppy nature and there is a real overtone of liquorice to the colour, taste and aftertaste of **Cascadian Black** (4.8%). There's more liquorice in the full-bodied **Belgian Red** (7.2%), given added complexity by black cherry and dried fruit, while **Triple Chocoholic** (4.8%) is a first-rate chocolate stout, with some interesting smoky coffee notes stirred into a beautifully soporific experience.

Saltaire Pride (3.9%)

It's entirely fitting that Salt's Mill, source of this village's growth and prosperity, should take pride of place on the label of the brewery's flagship ale, which packs in sufficient spice and hops to suggest you are drinking something rather stronger.

It pours an attractive golden colour with a firm and persistent creamy head that perhaps masks some of the aroma. But it really asserts itself on the palate, an insistent dry and grapefruity bitterness zings across the tongue, aided by some refreshing effervescence.

This classic English pale bitter derives its spicy fruitiness from a melange of Challenger, Bramling Cross and Cascade hops and was a silver prizewinner in the 2014 World Beer Awards. Like most of the Saltaire beers, it's widely available.

Samuel Smith's Brewery

The Old Brewery, High Street, Tadcaster, North Yorkshire, LS24 9SB;
T: 01937 832225; W: www.samuelsmithsbrewery.co.uk

Fiercely, determinedly – sometimes maddeningly – traditional, Yorkshire's oldest brewery continues to plough its own distinctive furrow. The beers are brewed with water from the 85-foot well sunk in 1758, fermented in slate squares with the same strain of yeast they used in Victorian times, and delivered to their vast estate of pubs in wooden casks. When you step into a Sam Smith's pub, whether in the north where there are many, or in London where there are several rather splendid ones, you are guaranteed only to find their own products – beers, wines, spirits, soft drinks. Don't ask for the guest beer because they won't have one.

Head for the creamy and malty **Old Brewery Bitter** (4%), the lighter but dryer, hoppier **Best Bitter** (3.7%) or the robust caramelly **Dark Mild** (2.8%) which has bags of taste, despite the shandy-level strength. It's worth exploring their bottles too. **Winter Welcome** (6%) is a sturdy seasonal ale, which comes in 550ml bottles, a characteristically curious measure, a drip short of an American pint and a splash short of an Imperial one. The design and recipe change every year – and it's one of the more expensive products on Sam Smith's keenly-priced menu.

Yorkshire Stingo (8%)

Crazy name, crazy beer. The label on this bottled beer is interesting, for a start, and looks like the kind of thing you might have found on an old bag of sticky toffees, just after the end of rationing. If the effect is deliberate then it's thoroughly appropriate, because despite having a rather undistinguished aroma, Stingo delivers a rich and unexpected blast of treacle as soon as it splashes across the tongue. It is during a year-long maturation period in oak casks that it develops the smooth rounded dried fruit and saffron flavours which beautifully disguise its strength. Only in a long and genuinely warming aftertaste do you get a sense of its true potency. Yorkshire Stingo would probably make a fantastic cold remedy, clearing the passageways while soothing the throat and warming the very cockles of your heart.

🏠 The Eagle Tavern, North Street, Leeds

There were once 11 pubs in North Street, serving tightly-packed terraced housing nearby. Gradually the houses went, and so did the pubs, until at this end of the street only the Eagle remained, hemmed in by factories, warehouses and five lanes of traffic.

I feared it was going the same way as its neighbours, but Samuel Smith's had other plans, spending 18 months on the painstaking resurrection of a business whose existence was held together by good wishes and grime. If there is a pub more patently deserving of such love so long withheld, then I have yet to find it.

Its two large rooms have been replaced by five intimate spaces, one of them with a long mahogany-panelled bar topped with fonts offering the whole Sam Smith's range. When I visited in December 2016, prices started at an astonishing £1.34 a pint. A sculpted golden eagle dominates the corridor where these five rooms meet, and where stairs lead to the 15 lavish bedrooms which have turned this simple drinkers' house into a quality hotel.

The Eagle once garnered awards for its real ale. Its current concentration on keg makes a return to those days unlikely, but the most diehard CAMRA member should rejoice that this once-threatened pub has been brought spectacularly back to life.

A Scarborough pub crawl

This circular route starts at the one-roomed micropub the **Stumble Inn** close to the railway station in Westborough, which features six guest ales, many local, and a whole host of craft ciders. From here, head back past the front of the station to reach the busy Wetherspoon pub **Lord Rosebery**. Continue along here before turning left into North Street where you will find the traditional town centre local **The Angel**.

From here, take a walk down towards the sea front. Just past the Brunswick shopping centre you'll find the sports-oriented **Hole in the Wall** in Vernon Road, which also has a decent beer garden. Head back up Vernon Road and into Somerset Terrace to find Yorkshire craft beers at the **Scholars Bar**. And from here it's a short hop back to the station.

North of the city centre, you'll find a great choice of ales, some brewed onsite, at the **North Riding Brewpub** in North Marine Road, a multi-award winning CAMRA favourite. Close to the front in Sandside, the **King Richard III** serves draught beers, often including choices from Wold Top Brewery (p180) – as well as hearty seaside food.

Scarborough Brewery

*Barry's Lane, Scarborough, YO12 4HA; T: 01723 367506;
E: scarboroughbrews@gmail.com;
W: www.scarboroughbrewery.co.uk*

Though of moderate strength, **Transmission** (3.9%) with its hoppy aroma and subtle citrus flavours is a perfect introduction to a coastal brewer which has, for the past seven years or so, been doing the simple things pretty well. There are some curious, perhaps slightly off-putting aromas to **Citra** (4.2%) but once on the palate its invigorating lemony flavours emerge. That fruit theme continues through the American-hopped golden ales **Sealord** (4.3%) and **Ship of Fools** (4.5%) and is given full voice in the golden, toffee-and-tropicals **Old Sailor** (4.9%). A muscular **Stout** (4.6%) shifts the emphasis into coffee, chocolate, smoke, toast and prunes; seasonals and occasionals fill out the range.

Sentinel Brewing

178 Shoreham St, Sheffield S1 4SQ;
T: 0114 399 9888;
W: www.sentinelbrewing.co

Visit the splendid taproom beside Sentinel Brewery and you can try the latest house beers in their sensuous curvy Craftmaster glassware. Beneath its high corrugated roof, painted brickwork and factory lighting embrace the building's industrial purpose, re-positioning it for social use. High glass windows divide drinkers from the steel brewing vessels and fermenting tanks; taps on the bar are primed with all the latest produce. With its generous, refreshing, rounded malt taste, **Sheffield Bitter** (3.3%) is an easy introduction to Sentinel; the ruby red **Cherry Porter** (5.5%) has a richer, more oily texture, a dusty dryness and just a suggestion of the fruit character suggested by the name, while the **Orange Stout** (4.2%) may be short on body, but has plenty of orange, dark chocolate and coffee to compensate. The list changes regularly.

Settle Brewery

Unit 2B, The Sidings Ind Est, Settle, BD24 9RP; T: 01729 824936;
W: www.settlebrewery.co.uk

The Settle-Carlisle line offers one of the most spectacular rail journeys in Britain. From the sidings close to Settle station, the town's brewery is providing some similarly dazzling sensory experiences. Its flagship craft products are the well-balanced and sessionable **Blonde** (3.6%) and the Yorkshire ale **Mainline** (3.8%) whose energetic hop quality is balanced by some moderate dark fruit sweetness. Yet beyond these fiercely traditional ales with their 'age of steam' pumpclips, Settle has stretched into the craft market with beers marketed under the Just The Ticket and Nine Standards labels – the latter formerly brewed in Cumbria. **Attermire** (4.2%) is a proper juicy, citric IPA yet brewed to a mundane, sessionable strength; **No3 Porter** (4.7%) is a jet black, creamy, smoky, coffee, caramel delight.

Nº4
NINE STANDARDS
AMBER ALE

A RICH MALTY AMBER ALE WITH
FRAGRANT HOPS, HINTS OF CITRUS
AND A SPICY NOSE

ABV 3.7%

CRAFT ALES BY SETTLE BREWERY

Nº3
NINE STANDARDS
PORTER

A CLASSIC ROBUST PORTER;
BLACK AND CREAMY, WITH A HEADY MIX OF
RICH CARAMEL AND COFFEE

ABV 4.7%

CRAFT ALES BY SETTLE BREWERY

Sheffield Brewery

Sheffield Brewery
J C Albyn Complex, Burton Road, Sheffield, S3 8BZ;
T: 0114 272 7256;
W: www.sheffieldbrewery.com

Joseph Pickering's Victorian silver polish business was symbiotic with Sheffield's burgeoning cutlery and silver plate industries. It expanded into furniture polish – then cornered the market with Blanco, a white polish used by the military for webbing, khaki and helments and by tennis and cricket players for their shoes and pads. Though the business finally closed in the 1960s, its echoes can still be felt in Sheffield Brewery, which now uses Pickering's abandoned factory premises. A little museum in the basement is a shrine to shine.

When the brewery moved in here in 2006, it had lain virtually undisturbed for 40 years, and I suspect that old Joseph would recognise something of himself in the industry of head brewer Dr Tim Stillman, who left a 25-year career in academe to turn his biochemistry to productive use: "I was in X-ray crystallography research and I enjoyed it, but there was always the pressure of having to apply for research grants."

And though his research now largely involves hops and malt, Tim says there are some important cross-overs between this and his former life. "There's a lot of science to this. You need exactly the right temperature and timing for the enzymes to go to work in the brew. Things can go wrong very quickly."

His core beers are right in the brewing mainstream. The first two he introduced were named after the city's defining geographical features – light, golden and very easy-going pale ale **Five Rivers** (3.8%) and the drier, hoppier and more determinedly bitter **Seven Hills** (4.1%). There's some nutty, caramelly goodness to the traditional Yorkshire best bitter **Crucible** (3.8%) while there's a dark, silky, chocolate and coffee complexity to **Sheffield Porter** (4.4%) which belies its moderate strength. With its Czech hops and lager

malt **Blanco Blonde** (4.2%) is an ale in name only.

Tim has spread his wings into some interesting specials which expand on the polish theme, like crisp and golden **Brightshine** (3.8%) and the aromatic, citric-sharp yet full-bodied hop bomb **Razor Paste** (5.6%). Some make their way into bottles; a tap room cheek-by-jowl with the brewhouse allows drinkers to see the latest beers taking shape.

Slightly Foxed Brewery

2 Richmond House, Caldene Business Park, Mytholmroyd, HX7 5QL;
T: 07412 008221; E: sales@slightlyfoxedbrewery.co.uk;
W: www.slightlyfoxedbrewery.co.uk

Like many now making a living from it, Simon Chantler began brewing at home, though few started so young: "I was only 14. I just used to brew on the stove."

He gradually expanded his operation after leaving home and the Slightly Foxed beers are all his homebrews, scaled up, including his entry level **Pale** (3.6%) which carries some nice American hop bite. Though "slightly foxed" is actually a term to describe the condition of pages in a second hand book, the brewery adapts it for a range of beers with distinctive fox-shaped pumpclips. "It gives you a lot of scope for the design," says Simon.

For his biggest seller, they gave the fox a hipster makeover with glasses, a checked shirt and moustache to denote that uber-pale **Crafty Fox** (4.1%) is their take on the craft ale trend, dry hopped for massive aroma.

For the future, he's considering really chasing the craft ale market. "We're talking about launching a sub-brand to do some more extreme beers and put them in kegs. I love Magic Rock. I had one of their beers called Custard Pie and it tasted just like custard! People like this are really pushing the envelope. There are some real challenges to your skills as a brewer to produce a very strong beer or to do something really innovative."

His strongest ales so far are the IPA **Bengal Fox** and the pale and sharply citric **Prairie Fox** (both 5.2%).

And he adds: "We are more about getting beer into the pubs. Without that there'd be no money coming in to let you do all the other interesting stuff."

And though the beer is widely distributed across South Yorkshire and Lancashire, a pop-up bar on the Mytholmroyd site allows locals to try the latest produce on Friday evenings. Simon sees this as an important way of staying in touch with what his hard work is actually all about: "The reason we do what we do is because we like to drink beer with other people. You can lose sight of that when you are just running it as a business."

Small World Beers

Unit 10, Barncliffe Business Park, Near Bank, Shelley, West Yorkshire, HD8 8LU; T: 01484 602805; E: info@smallworldbeers.com; W: www.smallworldbeers.com

A natural spring in the picturesque Barncliffe Valley provides the liquor for this 20-barrel brewery established in 2013. Beers include the crisp and golden **Barncliffe Bitter** (3.7%), the more noticeably citric and hoppy **Spike's Gold** (4.4%) and the more full-bodied fruity pale **Twin Falls** (5.2%) though the standout beer is the dry and toasty **Thunderbridge Stout** (5.2%) which derives its sweetness from chocolate malts. A changing roster of seasonals and specials keeps things interesting; the golden **Winter Bank** (4%) draws surprising mango notes from its left-field hop combination.

A clutch of fine pubs – the Three Acres in Roydhouse, Flying Ferret in Shelley and the Woodman in Thunderbridge – in the picturesque, rolling valleys between Huddersfield and Barnsley, each stock Small World beers.

Stancill Brewery

Unit 2, Oakham Drive, Sheffield, S3 9QX; T: 0114 275 2788;
E: tom@stancillbrewery.co.uk; W: www.stancillbrewery.co.uk

When lifelong friends Tom Gill and Adam Hague salvaged brewing kit from the closed-down Oakwell Brewery, they were also able to save a legendary beer eulogised by celebrity locals such as Parky and Dickie Bird. Tom and Adam persuaded Oakwell's head brewer Jonny Stancill to join them at the new venture in Sheffield and even put his name over the door. The reborn dark amber **Barnsley Bitter** (3.8%) with its softly-spoken malt and caramel character was immediately named Champion Beer of Yorkshire. Stancill beers also include earthy mild **Stancill Black** (3.7%), the light and floral **Stainless** (4.3%) and the crisp clean **Sheffield Pilsner** (5%) brewed with soft Peak District water and hops from Germany and the Czech Republic.

A local legend

🍺 Barnsley Bitter

For a beer of such uncomplicated beauty, the history of Barnsley Bitter is a surprisingly complex one. In the immediate post-war years, Barnsley Bitter's popularity grew from the mining communities of south Yorkshire to become a national phenomenon. In the seventies, **Barnsley Brewery** was taken over by Courage and closed down, before **Oakwell Brewery** started brewing a version in the 1990s from a unit on the same site.

Also during the late 90's another Barnsley Bitter was being brewed at **Barnsley Brewing** in Elsecar, though the writing was on the wall for that one when the brewery closed and production was switched to **Blackpool Brewery** – a move unlikely to find favour in Yorkshire. Meanwhile, Dave Hughes, who had been head brewer at Elsecar, set up **Acorn** brewery, whose own Barnsley Bitter has now become a local favourite.

Oakwell closed in 2013, paving the way for the establishment of **Stancill**, who now brew their own Barnsley Bitter. In Sheffield.

Steel City Brewing

The Circle, 33 Rockingham Lane, Sheffield, S1 4FW;
E: dave@steelcitybrewing.co.uk; W: www.steelcitybrewing.co.uk

Though it's common practice now, Steel City were among the UK's first cuckoo brewers – holding their own licence but creating their beers on other brewers' kit. Still cuckoos, still irregular, Steel City's one-off beers are a rare find; though Shakespeare's, The Rutland and Devonshire Cat are probably your best bet in Sheffield, while York's Woolpack and Huddersfield's Corner take them a little farther afield.

A heavyweight collaboration with Bristol's Arbor and Wales's Hopcraft spawned the jet-black, bottle-conditioned monster that is **Argy Bargy** (10.4%). This rich, oily barley wine has a fresh aroma of wet woodland, and on the palate there is so much rich, thick malt, black coffee and the purest dark chocolate that you can actually taste the blackness.

Steampunk Brewery

29 Hillcrest Drive, Allerton Bywater, WF10 3QW; T: 07789 988077;
E: neil.sherburn@sky.com

A chance conversation with the landlady of the Lion at Castleford persuaded Neil Sherburn to turn his homebrew hobby into a small business. A fabricator by trade, he built his own nine-barrel kit which now produces occasional beers both for the pub and for local beer festivals, the brewery name honouring a genre of science fiction Gothic. When we spoke in February 2017, he was just planning the recipe for his first permanent flagship beer **Blacker Namba**, the name a tribute to the black-and-amber Castleford Tigers.

Stod Fold Brewing

Ogden, Halifax, HX2 8XL; T: 01422 245951;
E: Paul@stodfoldbrewing.com; W: www.stodfoldbrewing.com

Given how their reputation has spread, it's surprising to learn that Stod Fold have only been around since 2015. Their four core ales have already gained quite a following, with distribution across a 40-mile radius of the brewery.

They include the simple refreshing **Gold** (3.8%), the more toffee-ish and substantial best bitter **Amber** (4.2%) and the yeasty, malty **Blonde** (4.5%). Their **Pils** (4.8%) is an accomplished cask ale take on the traditional central European style.

Summer Wine Brewery

Unit 15, Crossley Mills, New Mill Road, Honley, Holmfirth HD9 6QB;
T: 01484 665466; E: info@summerwinebrewery.co.uk;
W: www.summerwinebrewery.co.uk

It's strange to think that the infantile misadventures of three elderly delinquents could have put a little Pennine town on the map, but much of Holmfirth's success as a tourist trap derives from the long-running TV series.

The Summer Wine brewery celebrates this connection, the very name conjuring images of wrinkle-stockinged crones and scruffy pensioners. Even so, the beers produced in this name bear little resemblance to the ones Compo, Clegg and Foggy would have been drinking at the White Horse. Oh sure, there's soft, roasty dark mild **Deliverance** (3.7%) and zingy pale ale **Zenith** (4%) but from here the catalogue careers off into the kind of upland adventures the trio might have appreciated.

There's bitter espresso stout **Barista** (4.8%), significantly hopped ruby red ale **Rouge** (5.8%) and the innovative **Cohort** (7.5%) which teams dark malt with US hops and Belgian yeast into a black rye ale. Even the double India Pale Ale **Maelstrom** (9%) is dangerously drinkable, but perhaps should be avoided if you're planning to spend the afternoon hurtling downhill in a bathtub.

Sunbeam Ales

Sunbeam Terrace, Leeds,
West Yorkshire, LS11 6EW;
T: 07772 002437;
E: nigelpoustie@yahoo.co.uk;
W: www.sunbeamales.co.uk

Had brewer Nigel Postie made his home in one of Leeds's less evocatively-named streets – South Accommodation Road or Grimthorpe Avenue maybe – he would probably have found some different way of naming his brewery. But when you live in Sunbeam Terrace and brew the beers in your garage, you may as well celebrate the address. He further honours the location with the zesty, citric **Born in LS11** (5.1%), one of his most popular ales. Others include juicy tropical fruit IPA **Sun Kissed** (3.7%), coffee and orange peel infused stout **Eclipse** (3.8%), and rich and creamy plummy porter **Thunder Road** (6.2%). Nigel's classic cloudy witbier **Foggy Morning** (5.1%), with its lemongrass and banana accents, was named Champion Beer at Leeds CAMRA beer festival in 2016.

A Leeds pub crawl

Though lacking the architectural magnificence of York, Leeds offers so fulsome an adventure for the determined pub crawler that there are whole books written about it.

This circular walk starts at the station concourse. On leaving the front entrance turn right to reach craft ale and charcuterie paradise **Friends of Ham**. Turn right into Boar Lane and follow it as far as Lower Briggate, where just across the bridge is the graceful sweeping curved frontage of the **Adelphi**, once the favourite of staff at nearby Tetley Brewery. Crossing back over the river and into Briggate, we reach the city's most unspoiled pub, the elegantly tiled and coppered **Whitelocks** and its stylish craft keg sidekick the **Turks Head**.

Further up Briggate we reach **North Bar**, an unprepossessing ribbon of a bar whose vision and innovation nonetheless proved a catalyst for the city's beer explosion. Just beyond here is cavernous music and pizza venue **Belgrave** which always has something to surprise in its choice of cask and keg. From here, head up Merrion Street, possibly calling in at the lively **Social**, and on into Great George Street to reach the wonderfully grandiose **Victoria**, all wooden panels, etched glass and almost endless hand-pulled choice.

From here head due south back towards the station, but don't get on board before visiting Mill Hill, where **Bundobust** offers a zeitgeist craft and curry experience.

Visits to the **Fox and Newt** (see p45), **Tapped** (p162-3), **North Brewing** (p120-1), **Northern Monk Refectory** (p124-5) and **Hungry Bear** (p90-91) each offer quite distinct takes on the brewpub experience. Just south of town the **Garden Gate** in Hunslet is a superbly preserved Victorian alehouse sadly hemmed in by charmless low-rise concrete.

The **Town Hall Tavern**, **Hop**, **Angel**, **Head of Steam** and **Mr Foleys** offer the chance to browse the range of out-of-town brewers Timothy Taylors, Ossett, Sam Smiths, Camerons and York respectively. South of the river, **The Cross Keys**, **Midnight Bell** (p102–3) and **Grove** (p55) offer a rewarding circuit of real ale gems.

Tapped Brew Co

Sheffield Station, Sheaf St, Sheffield, S1 2BP; T: 0114 273 7558;
and 51 Boar Lane, Leeds LS1 5EL; T: 0113 2441953;
E: info@tappedbrewco.com; W: www.tappedbrewco.com

Dave Sanders is one of the legends of the Yorkshire brewing scene. After cutting his teeth at the old Feast and Firkin brewpub in Leeds more than 20 years ago, stints at Elland, Kirkstall, Saltaire and Copper Dragon breweries followed, before he took on the job of overseeing production at Tapped's two breweries late in 2016. We meet at the Leeds branch and I watch Dave busying himself with his daily routines before he finds time to chat at one of the tables beneath the pipes which cross the ceiling, carrying the beer from the shiny brewkit to their 1,500-litre serving tanks beside the bar.

Despite his experience, Dave admits he's on something of a learning curve: "It's a completely different system here, I'm still getting my head around it." The Tapped brewkit is a decoction brewery, a system commonly used for making lager in Germany and the Czech Republic, but rare in the UK. "It's not something I had ever done before," says Dave. "But so far, so good."

His job will involve maintaining some of the great beers which have made Tapped such a popular destination, while introducing some new ones. So he's been getting to grips with brewing a wheat beer – another personal first – and trying to develop some new ideas, both here at the keg brewery and at the cask ale plant in Sheffield.

Beers include the cloudy amber **Rodeo** (4%), sweet but potent American-influenced IPA **Bullet** (5.9%) and spicy, bubblegum wheat beer **Miami Weisse** (5.5%).

It's autumn, and Dave is keen to show off Tapped's annual brew of the assertive, full-flavoured and characterful **Hop Harvest Lager** (6.2%) which features fresh green hops pitched into the brew just hours after they're picked on an East Yorkshire farm. "It's unfiltered, unpasteurised, and to all intents and purposes it's a real ale – but there are still plenty of CAMRA diehards who wouldn't drink it."

Perhaps unwittingly, Dave has returned to a theme which has been exercising brewers, bartenders and beer-tickers for the past decade and more – what exactly is "craft ale"? It is a term which has defied all sensible attempts at definition, though I quite like Dave's analogy: "It's a bit like jazz. It's hard to explain what it is and what it isn't, but when you hear it, you know it's jazz."

Tapped's quintet of Yorkshire bars – Leeds, Harrogate, Sheffield and York Tap, plus Pivni, also in York – are the ideal places to sample Dave's wares. If you must head south, the Euston Tap holds similar delights.

T&R Theakston Brewery

The Brewery, Masham, Ripon, HG4 4YD; T: 01765 680000;
E: info&bookings@theakstons.co.uk; W: www.theakstons.co.uk

Visitors are welcomed daily to Robert Theakston's tower brewery – the third site used for brewing since it had begun in 1827, but still in use today.

Beer has been in constant production here since 1875; all of it passes through the original Victorian mash tun. One copper vessel is a relatively new addition, having been installed in 1936, though it was second hand, even then. Dry and golden **Best Bitter** (3.8%) is a quintessential Yorkshire ale, bright and golden **Lightfoot** (4.1%) has some gentle peachy flavours, while late hopping with Golding hops gives **Black Bull** (3.9%) a pronounced hoppy edge. Keg, craft keg and a host of seasonal beers fill out the roster.

There is something faintly pantomimic about it, yet Theakston and neighbours Black Sheep remain fierce rivals, not least because of the bloodline which links the two family-owned brewers.

As with their neighbours, Theakston beers are widely available across the county.

Tarn 51 Brewing

Robin Hood, 10 Church Road, Altofts, WF6 2NJ; T: 01924 892911;
E: realale@tarn51brewing.co.uk; W: www.tarn51brewing.co.uk

The Robin Hood, Wakefield CAMRA's pub of the year in 2015, is probably the best place to sample the produce from Tarn 51's three-barrel brewery which is housed in a shipping container out back.

Brewing only started in 2016, but already the beers have started to make their way into the free trade across the county. They include the simple, sessionable pine and citrus IPA **Lady Cluck** (4%) and the very dark surprisingly liquoricey **Appy As A Pig In Stout** (4.2%).

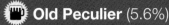 Old Peculier (5.6%)

Sales of some big name beers are suffering in an over-crowded marketplace, yet those few with the history and cachet of Old Peculier should comfortably survive. The words "The Legend" on the label are fully justified. From its peculiar spelling to the town's seal of a crimson-clad Roger de Mowbray kneeling in apparent supplication, Theakston Old Peculier is every inch a Yorkshire legend.

This deep red-brown ale has less of a significant aroma than you might expect from a beer of 5.6% ABV, and yet it more than compensates with a full-on assault on the palate. Smooth and full-bodied, it blends rich, dried fruit, Christmas cake flavours with the woody, grainy, almost nutty nature of the malts and caramels and just a suggestion of black pepper, which persists into a long aftertaste that develops in sufficient bitterness to make you eager to down still more. To taste it is to commune with history.

Three Peaks Brewery

7 Craven Terrace, Settle, BD24 9DB; T: 01729 822939

Three easy-going and appropriately named beers are the core products for Yorkshire's westernmost brewery, originally established by Colin and Susan Ashwell in the cellar of their home. These are vanilla accented **Pen-Y-Ghent** bitter (3.8%); light and insubstantial **Ingleborough Gold** (4%) and the slightly darker more assertive **Whernside Pale** (4.2%). A number of occasional beers augment the selection; in 2016 a sturdy, oily Boatman's Stout (5%) was launched to mark the bicentenary of the Leeds-Liverpool Canal.

Three Fiends Brewhouse

Brookfield Farm, Mill Moor Road, Meltham, Holmfirth, HD9 5LN;
T: 07810 370430; E: sales@threefiends.co.uk;
W: www.threefiends.co.uk

They're friends as well as fiends. The trio who set up this new brewery in 2015 had first met at school aged 11. They scored an early success when spicy and distinctly orangey **Bad Uncle Barry** pale ale (4.2%) was named Best Bitter at Huddersfield's Oktoberfest in 2016. The big tasting malty pale ale **Boomer** (4.3%) makes good use of hops from Australia and New Zealand, while **Moko Titi** (4.5%) is a premium session IPA, with peachy tastes to the forefront. A brewery so named inevitably produces something fiendish – **Voodoo** (6%) is a rich double chocolate stout with a surprising late kick of chilli; **Dark Side** (5.3%) a smooth black IPA. You'll find several of these in bottle, and kegging was due to start in 2017.

Tigertops Brewery

22 Oakes Street, Flanshaw, Wakefield, WF2 9LN;
T: 01924 897728; E: tigertopsbrewery@hotmail.com

One website lists over 230 different brews created by this innovative brewery, which was established by Stewart and Lynda Johnson, now of the Foxfield brewpub in Cumbria. Their friend Barry Smith is now the brewer; his day job cutting trees and verges for the local council has earned him the nickname Axeman.

Yorkshire Dales Pubs

Regular outlets for Three Peaks include the **Golden Lion** in Horton and the **Talbot** in Settle, as well as several over the border into Lancashire. But the wonderful varied pubs right across the Yorkshire Dales bring an alcoholic flavour to this broad bucolic landscape, and a whole book could easily be devoted to this area alone.

Each of the major towns and villages of the Dales has at least one pub to recommend it. In Hawes this would be the attractive **White Hart,** where the beer is sourced from local breweries, the meat from a nearby farm. The triple-bay fronted **Golden Lion** dominates one side of Leyburn's market square. It's a similar tale in Masham, where the rather grand **King's Head** serves ales from both the town's great breweries, though Theakston's would recommend the **White Bear**, the only pub they own – and it's right beside their rival Black Sheep Brewery, for spicy, provocatively good measure.

Askrigg's three pubs – the **White Rose**, **Crown Inn** and **Kings Arms** – can all be relied on to serve beers from the Yorkshire Dales Brewing Company.

Others recommended by contributors to this book include the **Craven Arms** at Appletreewick, **Cross Keys** at Bellerby. **Fountain Hotel** at Hawes. **Bolton Arms** at Redmire, **Old Hill** at Ingleton, **Fox and Hounds** at West Witton, **Farmers Arms** at Muker, **George and Dragon** at Aysgarth, **Tempest Arms** in Elslack, **Red Lion** at Burnsall and **Lister Arms** in Malham. Personally, I have a certain fondness for the fiercely traditional **Buck Inn** in Thornton Watlass, just north of Masham. At the heart of the village is a wide green which doubles as a pasture for the cows and as a cricket pitch for the local team. The stone fronted pub sits just beyond the boundary; Tony and Vicky Jowett bought The Buck in 2014 and have worked hard to restore its reputation for hearty Yorkshire hospitality.

The Golden Lion at Leyburn

Timothy Taylor Brewery

Knowle Spring Brewery, Keighley, BD21 1AW; T: 01535 603139;
E: tim@timtaylors.co.uk; W: www.timothytaylor.co.uk

When beautifully-balanced, sessionable **Boltmaker** (4%) was named Champion Beer of Britain in 2014, you could forgive one or two southern brewers for groaning inwardly, while generously applauding the Keighley brewery's success. This flagship prize, awarded annually on the opening day of the Great British Beer Festival, is highly-coveted in the industry, guaranteeing the winner national exposure – and a huge spike in sales. And Timmy Taylor's is by far the most successful brewery in these awards. Their iconic **Landlord** (4.3%) has been Champion Beer of Britain four times

and runner-up on three occasions. Natural Pennine spring water forms the basis for these world famous beers, which also include a sweet and toffee-ish **Dark Mild** (3.5%), a zesty and palate-cleansing **Golden Best** (3.5%) and the rich, caramelly **Ram Tam** (4.3%).

🏠 The Fleece, Main Street, Haworth

Any Timothy Taylor pub is worth a visit, but combining a couple of these iconic beers with a day out in lovely, historic Haworth seems a fine use of anybody's time. The Fleece sits alongside Haworth's dramatically sloping cobbled main street and as you step in from the Victorian streetscape, the long bar is dead ahead with the pub's main drinking and dining spaces down to your left. A wood burning stove between two of the rooms provides light, heat and that splendid feeling of cosy intimacy. The decor is dominated by shades of coffee, cream and chocolate, while heavy curtains, interesting lanterns on the ceilings and windowsills and some archive photographs of old Haworth each lend a sense of antiquity to the place.

The pub used to share the premises with the local brass band, but now they have upped tubas and left, creating extra space where Taylors plan to extend their bed and breakfast accommodation from the existing seven rooms to ten.

Legend has it that Branwell Bronte drank here too; some say the ghost of the writers' ill-starred artist brother lingers here still.

Toolmakers Brewery

6-8 Botsford Street, Sheffield, S3 9PF; T: 01142 454374;
E: info@toolmakersbrewery.com; W: www.toolmakersbrewery.com

The toolmaking theme is entirely appropriate to an area steeped in steelmaking, and a whole host of beers build on that theme. Munich malt adds some caramel to **Lynchpin** (4%), while there are some sweet-toothed suggestions of chocolate and liquorice to **Toffee Hammer** (4.3%) and some floral aromas to the citric **Sonic Screw Driver** (4.2%). The on-site bar is both a brewery tap and a party venue available for hire.

Treboom Brewery

Millstone Yard, Main Street, Shipton-by-Beningbrough, YO30 1AA;
T: 01904 471569; E: info@treboom.co.uk; W: www.treboom.co.uk

Treboom marries the talents of York University research scientist John Lewis and Royal College of Art ceramicist Jane Blackman into a brewery of style and innovation. Their flagship beer is the ghostly pale, affably citric and nicely carbonated **Yorkshire Sparkle** (4%) while **Kettle Drum** (4.3%) is a more substantial, darker best bitter, and **Hop Britannia** (5%) celebrates the best of our home-grown hops in a deep golden ale with pronounced berry and currant notes. In the specials and seasonals a restless imaginative spirit emerges – the honey and pomegranate **Sekhmet** (4%), the green-hopped **Kettle Drum** (4.3%) packed with freshly-picked hops grown on site, the Yorkshire Saison **Maillot Blanc** (4.8%) and the wheat beer **Myricale** (5%) which is flavoured with foraged bog myrtle.

Trinity Brewing Company

Belle Vue Stadium, Doncaster Road, Wakefield, WF1 5EY;
T: 07963 435552; E: sales@trinitybrewing.co.uk;
W: www.trinitybrewery.co.uk

In the disused toilet block in one corner of Wakefield's rugby league stadium, something truly remarkable is taking place. Using redundant kit salvaged and refurbished, enthusiasts Neil Land and Steve Locking created a five barrel plant in the confines of 20 square feet – and with the support of former Tetley man Steve Chapman have started producing some fine ales, both for the rugby fans and drinkers further afield. Several have an obvious sporting theme like grapefruity **Hop and Under** (4.2%), golden **Belle Vue Blonde** (4.2%), gentle red ale **Ruby League** (3.6%) and the honey-accented **Bee-tween The Sticks** (4.2%). Pale ale **Well I'll be Foxed** (3.9%) honours Trinity legend Neil Fox.

True North Brewing

47 Eldon Street, Sheffield S1 4GY; T: 0114 272 0569;
E: info@truenorthbrewco.uk; W: www.truenorthbrewco.uk

After four years using others' kit, True North finally found a home in Sheffield city centre in 2016. The recent installation of a brewery bar and new tanks to increase capacity and output of keg beers **True North Pilsner** (5%) and **Session IPA** (3.9%) are surely signs of a confident operation on the up. Cask beers include malty amber **Best Bitter** (3.8%), sweetish fruity **Red Rye** (4.7%) and golden vanilla **Blonde** (4%).

Twisted Angel Brewing

North Newbald; T: 07432 588159; E: twistedangelbrewing@hotmail.co.uk;
W: www.twistedangelbrewing.com

Plans to turn an old hearse into a mobile bar will add an extra point of distinction for this East Yorkshire operation, which established itself in 2015 as a cuckoo brewer with Brass Castle. The first brew, massively hopped, orange-amber IPA **Berserker** (7.5%), threw down a telling marker – blasting drinkers with heroic levels of citric hop in the aroma and bitterness on the palate. Now operating on his own kit, brewer Matthew Hall has added the stout **Daywalker** (5.8%), golden bitter **Impaler** (5.1%) and pale ale **Medusa** (4%) to the list.

Two Roses Brewery

Unit 9, Darton Business Park, Barnsley Road, Darton, Barnsley, S75 5QX;
T: 07780 701254; E: enquiries@tworosesbrewery.co.uk;
W: www.tworosesbrewery.co.uk

Though mothballed for a while as owner James Taylor tackled serious illness, recent activity on social media suggests that Two Roses now seems to be right back in business. His wife's micropub the Arcade Alehouse in Barnsley is probably the best place to check on progress.

Vocation Brewery

8 Craggs Country Business Park, New Road, Cragg Vale, Hebden Bridge, HX7 5TT; T: 01422 410 810; E: sales@vocationbrewery.com; W: www.vocationbrewery.com

Long-time beer obsessive John Hickling was a founding partner in Nottingham's Blue Monkey Brewery, and after stepping away from that project, realised he missed the challenge and craft of brewing – and established Vocation in his new home town of Hebden Bridge. Since then, punchy, hop-forward beers such as the dry hopped **Bread & Butter** (3.9%) and the black IPA **Divide & Conquer** (6.5%) have struck a chord with drinkers both in the UK and on export to Spain, France, the Netherlands and Ireland. Three new fermenters have raised capacity to around 30,000 pints per week. Other regular beers include tropical fruit American pale ale **Pride & Joy** (5.3%) and citric IPA **Heart & Soul** (4.4%). No two brews of Vocation's "ever-changing pale" **Chop & Change** (4.5%) are ever the same, as the hop variety changes with each brew. Many are available in can.

Hebden Bridge and Sowerby Bridge

The best place to get Vocation beer as fresh as possible is in their home town of Hebden Bridge. Regular stockists include the **Old Gate**, **Calan's Micro-Pub** and **Chapter 17**. The town's live music and socialism venue the **Trades Club** attracts star names, while just along the road in Sowerby Bridge, a short walk along the main street brings you from the pints-and-pizzas **Firehouse** to Ossett Brewery's **Shepherd's Rest** by way of the stone-flagged riverside **Turk's Head** and Thai food and pub fusion **Williams Bar**. The **Jubilee Refreshment Room** brings hand-pulled sustenance to passengers waiting at the railway station.

Wensleydale Brewery

Unit F, Manor Farm, Bellerby, North Yorkshire, DL8 5QH;
T: 01969 622463; E: enquiries@wensleydalebrewery.co.uk;
W: www.wensleydalebrewery.co.uk

Friends Geoff Southgate and Carl Gehrman started working at the brewery while they were still at school; when they took over in 2013 they were two of the youngest brewery owners in the UK at 23 and 22 respectively. Their entry-level **Bitter** (3.7%) offers the familiar Yorkshire bitter balance of malt and hop, while the slightly stronger **Falconer** (3.9%) delivers more distinct orange character. **Semer Water** (4.1%) transmits pronounced citrus in both aroma and taste, while **Black Dub** (4.4%) is a luxuriant, silky smooth oatmeal stout. Several are also available in bottle.

The George and Dragon, Hudswell

I found Wensleydale Falconer on the bar of this pub whose local fame spread nationwide in 2017 when it received CAMRA's much-coveted national pub of the year title. It's a far cry from 2008 when, like many village inns which struggled to make ends meet, the George and Dragon was forced to close down altogether. But with the support of the local community it re-opened just two years later and is now the absolute hub of village life – a shop, a library and a home for the local allotments. The six handpulls offer a changing choice of five real ales and one craft cider, while the kitchen turns out some hearty Yorkshire dishes. A beer garden commands spectacular views of the valley behind the pub; pictures inside show off a visit by the Prince of Wales.

Wharfedale Brewery

16, Church Street, Ilkley, LS29 9DS;
T: 07710 491217;
E: info@wharfedalebrewery.com;
W: www.wharfedalebrewery.com

The quaint, stone flagged Flying Duck in the town centre is the best place to appraise the produce of a brewery which was set up in 2012 and remains rather in the shadow of the longer-established Ilkley Brewery. Beers include the soft velvety mild **Black** (3.7%) which has some of the taste and texture of a strong but milky coffee; the refreshing, palate cleansing **Blonde** (3.9%) and the traditional, toffee-ish **Bitter** (3.9%). Despite being the Wharfedale brewpub, its bar still made room for local rivals Great Heck, Isaac Poad and Naylors on my recent visit.

An Ilkley Pub Crawl

The moorside town boasts an enviable clutch of watering holes, most of them clustered close enough to its central intersection to present an itinerary which is long on pubs and short on actual crawl-time.

Dominating this junction is the handsome, slightly forbidding **Crescent**, whose hotel bar offers alarmingly better choice than many; non-residents are definitely welcome. Close behind here is **The Yard**, which can usually be relied on to offer Ilkley Brewery ales.

Just along Church Street is the comfortable and foody **Black Hat**, whose name denotes a local cricket rivalry, and across the road is the town's first brewpub, the **Flying Duck** (see left). Further along here, take a left to reach the **Bar T'at,** one of the reliable Market Town Taverns. From here head uphill to Wells Road to reach **Friends of Ham**, a second venue for the craft beer and charcuterie business which has proved such a hit in Leeds.

Whippet Brewing

Unit 9, Brown Place, Leeds, LS11 0EF; T: 07928 101783;
E: sales@whippetbrewing.beer; W: www.whippetbrewing.beer

Whippet is based a short dog-walk from Leeds United's ground and founder Sam Parker admits that they initially thought about calling it Elland Road Brewery, but realised quickly that this could limit sales in Bradford, Huddersfield, Sheffield and Hull. So Whippet it became, namechecking not just a Yorkshire canine icon, but also the old elliptical greyhound stadium which once stood just across from the football ground.

Sam's passion has always been for beer, rather than for dogs. He gave up his job as a call centre manager for The Halifax seven years ago to become a full-time beer writer, penning articles for a number of magazines, and helping to promote Wetherspoon's among other things. It was only a matter of time before he turned his hand to brewing, and after briefly flirting with taking up the reins at Ridgeside Brewery in Meanwood, following the death of our mutual friend, head brewer Simon Bolderson, Sam chose instead to strike out on his own.

Unlike those newcomers intent on loading up their recipes with sackloads of hops to generate Herculean levels of bitterness the Whippet beers are straight up Yorkshire ales, utterly worthy of the honest, hard-working dog's name.

Each has a canine theme. They include the entry-level bitter **House Dogge** (3.7%), an easy-drinking bright copper session ale with gentle bitterness and dry finish; pale and golden **English Whippet** (4.8%) which has more obvious bitterness yet still the solid malty backdrop of a Yorkshire ale and **Snap Dog** (5.7%) is a rich and full bodied IPA which features a brace of New Zealand hops. Blonde **Flying Start** (4.5%) was specially brewed to raise funds for the Retired Greyhounds Trust.

If you need your beers to radiate infusions of elderflower, be as cloyingly thick as a chocolate orange or as cheek-suckingly citric as an ice-cold grapefruit, drink elsewhere, there's plenty of them about. But not here.

🍺 Little Curre (5.2%)

It is an accident of history, politics and geography that the United Kingdom's market for stout should have become utterly dominated by a brand from the Irish Republic.

I've always been partial to a pint of Guinness – and, in my youth, to very occasionally dunking cheese and onion crisps into the creamy head. But the choice for stout lovers across the country is now far greater, as new brewers have entered the market and rediscovered a love for this ancient brewing style, and sometimes stretched the envelope with the addition of chocolate, coffee and treacle for fresh variety.

At the same time, landlords have also discovered the cost benefits of stocking a cask of locally-produced stout rather than a keg of the uber-expensive Irish stuff.

Little Curre is Whippet's take on the genre. At 5.2% it's a tad stronger than some in the market, and that extra potency reveals itself in a full-bodied, silky, dark, smoky, mysterious ale. Whippet add roasted barley and flaked oatmeal to the brew, creating still more substance and smoothness.

Whitby Brewery

East Cliff, Whitby, YO22 4JR. T: 01947 228871;
E: info@whitby-brewery.com; W: www.whitby-brewery.com

Established in a tiny plant in 2013, Whitby Brewery has undergone a programme of expansion and relocated to a hand-built 20-barrel brewery and micropub in the shadow of Whitby Abbey on a rugged headland overlooking the North Sea; brewery tours start soon. Three of the cask ales are also available in bottle: the zesty and refreshing light ale **Abbey Blonde** (4.2%), the fruity but not over-bitter **Whitby Whaler** (4%) and toffee-ish liquorice-accented porter **Jet Black** (4.5%). Others include the full-bodied ruby ale **Saltwick Nab** (4.2%), passion fruit and grapefruity **IPA** (5.2%) and the **Black Death** (5%) stout, a favourite on Whitby's twice-a-year Goth Weekends, when the town is overrun by black-clad seekers of darkness and Dracula.

Whitechapel – see Halifax Steam Brewery

Wilde Child Brewing

Kirkstall, LS5 3NQ;
T: 07908 419028;
E: info@wildechildbrewing.co.uk;
W: www.wildechildbrewing.co.uk

In the short time since Keir McAllister-Wilde established his brewery in a Leeds garage, scaling up his home brews into a commercial operation, Wilde Child has gained an enviable reputation for its imaginative, high-quality cask, keg and bottled ales which are making their way into pubs and specialist beer stores across the county. Examples include the slightly sweet IPA **Outside The Box** (5.7%) which derives its citric nature from a generous dose of mandarins; sturdy, French-hopped amber ale **Enfant Terrible** (4.3%) and the indulgently chocolatey **Hedonistic Existence** (6.3%). As his beers get stronger, Keir allows his imagination to run wild both with the names and the recipes.

They include his firm black IPA **Hades Beckons** (6.66%), the bourbon stout **Instant Hobo** (9%), the doppelbock **Creature of Doom** (8.2%) and the slightly rough-at-the-edges spice and tropical fruit beast of an IPA which he has named **Hopstrosity** (10.5%).

179

Wishbone Brewery

2A Chesham St, Keighley, BD21 4LG; T: 01535 600412;
E: info@wishbonebrewery.co.uk;
W: www.wishbonebrewery.co.uk

The simple wishbone emblem on diamond-shaped pumpclips ensures products from this new brewery stand out on the bar. They include the grainy, earthy **Blonde** (3.6%), roasty, toasty stout **Abyss** (4.3%) and the significantly hopped dry and fruit-juicey American IPA **Divination** (5.6%). Their micky-taking pale cask ale **Pastiche** (3.7%) features three fashionable hop varieties and is a response to SIBA's efforts to provide a definition for craft ale. "It roughly proves the fact that to a certain extent the hops you use – or can get hold of if you have enough money – guide what beers get highly rated by drinkers," says brewer Adrian Chapman. "It shows how fickle the market for en-vogue hop flavours is, you could make two technically correct beers but the one with Citra, Simcoe and Galaxy will rate more highly."

Wold Top Brewery

Hunmanby Grange, Wold Newton, Driffield, YO25 3HS ;
T: 01723 892222 ;
E: enquiries@woldtopbrewery.co.uk;
W: www.woldtopbrewery.co.uk

Wold Top Brewery was founded in 2003 by Tom and Gill Mellor on their 600-acre farm high on the Yorkshire Wolds. They use home-grown barley and water gently filtered by wolds chalk and drawn from the farm's own borehole. There is a focus on sustainability and maintaining biodiversity, and on sourcing ingredients from nearby. The brewery predominantly supplies pubs in its own locality, though their handpulled beers are becoming an increasingly common sight on bars across the county – and you'll find their bottles in the supermarkets too.

Fragrant **Wold Top Bitter** (3.7%) is the entry-level ale, while others include firm and full-bodied ruby ale **Headland Red** (4.3%) and golden summer beer **Wold Gold** (4.8%), a winner at the 2016 World Beer Awards.

Thankfully devoid of parsley, sage, rosemary and thyme, the excellent **Scarborough Fair** (6%) is a beautifully sparkling golden IPA with some fruity aromas and a taste whose bitterness mellows into spicy vanilla and black cherry.

 Anglers' Reward (4%)

This golden, sessionable ale is a gentle, easy-going refresher, with some quite perfumy aromas, and an interesting, quite complex taste of biscuit, caramel and bags of citrus fruit. Its genuine bitter character is derived from a combination of Cascade and Goldings hops in the brew; the hoppy, bitter finish hangs around for a while too.

East Riding pubs

The benign, rolling and unfolding hills and vales of East Yorkshire are roughly bounded by the Humber Estuary, the Vale of York and the coast. Many of the quiet villages on this green, fecund landscape have pubs well worth visiting; many serve beers from local brewers. Beyond Hull – which has plenty of pub crawl opportunities (see p185) – the largest town is Bridlington, where the **Marine Bar** is a local favourite and regularly offers Wold Top beers. Beverley has a well-established drinking circuit with pubs such as **Monk's Walk**, the **Windmill**, **Dog and Duck**, **Grosvenor Club**, **Potting Shed** and **Chequers Micropub**. Samuel Smith's ancient gas-lit **White Horse** is a local legend, and universally known as **Nellie's**.

Others recommended by the breweries which have contributed to this book include **Pocklington Arts Centre**, the **Butcher's Dog** in Driffield, **New Inn** in Tickton, **Carpenters** and **Weighton Whippet** in Market Weighton and Hornsea's **Stackhouse Bar**.

York Brewery

12 Toft Green, York, YO1 6JT; T: 01904 621162;
E: enquiries@york-brewery.co.uk; W: www.york-brewery.co.uk

Founded in 1996, York have built a steady reputation through their core beers and a small string of interesting, well-run pubs, including Foley's Tap House in Leeds, named Best Cider Pub at 2016's Great British Pub Awards. Distribution remains concentrated on Yorkshire and Lancashire – and apparently a pint of York Brewery beer is now consumed every 23 seconds. Fruity, creamy **Blonde** (3.9%) and golden, bitter **Yorkshire Terrier** (4.2%) are among their big sellers. Several of the brewery ales namecheck this historic city's ancient past – **Centurion's Ghost** (5.4%) is a dark, smooth and mellow roasted ale, crisp and fruity **Legion IX** is their premium pale ale, while there is a rich fruitcake maltiness to high-octane dark ale **Imperium** (7.5%).

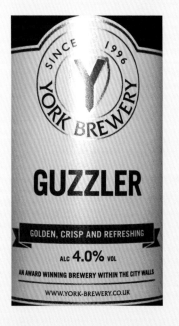

 Guzzler

Crisp, dry and refreshing Guzzler is very much the York Brewery session beer, whether it's the 4% version in bottle or the 3.6% brew which they send to the pubs. It's the essence of an easy-drinking pale ale, with a suggestion of tangerine in the aroma, a crisp blast of fresh fruit with a touch of carbonation and a slight buttery silkiness, before a dusty dryness emerges right at the finish, just tempting you to drink some more. And at this very moderate strength, why wouldn't you?

Mr Foley's Alehouse is a Leeds outpost for York Brewery

Yorkshire Brewing

Brewery Wharf, 70 Humber Street,
Hull, HU1 1TU; T: 01482 618000;
E: info@yorkshirebrewing.co.uk;
W: www.yorkshirebrewing.co.uk

Close to Hull's historic waterfront, in former fruit market warehouses rediscovered by the city's burgeoning Arts Quarter, Yorkshire Brewing is going from strength to strength, with capacity going through a four-fold increase in 2016-17. The sizeable range includes multi-hopped **Oregon Gold** (4.5%) with its notably refreshing melon aftertaste; sessionable hoppy and bitter **Mosaic** (4.2%) whose tangerine, berry and tropical fruit notes demonstrate the dimensions of this popular hop variety; and west coast influenced IPA **Waverider** (5.5%). There is clearly a thirst for innovation at work here: the dark, coffee-ish **Mutiny** (4.2%) blends oats and a host of malts in a 1750 London Porter recipe; rum adds to the complexity of dark seasonal ale **Old Ebenezer** (4.5%); while **Polar Beer** (6%) gains its oaky, rich fruity taste from maturation in old bourbon casks. And there's an eagerness to cast fresh fruit into the brewkit – fresh blackberries enrich **Blackjack** stout (4.5%), soft summer fruits enhance Belgian-influenced **Strawberry Blonde** (4.8%) and **Raspberry Tipple** (4.8%), oranges add extra spike to wheat beer **Moondance** (4.5%).

A Hull pub crawl

The City of Kingston-Upon-Hull allows inquisitive pub crawlers both to commune with the area's rich seafaring past – and to experience its modern, vibrant self, and the confidence which helped it become a European City of Culture in 2017.

This linear walk starts underground, at cellar bar **The Hop and Vine** in Albion Street, with its changing choice of local beers, plus some rare ciders and perries. From here trek eastwards to the old town to find the very traditional **City Hotel** with its grand carved stone frontage and the lively events centre **Kardomah 94**.

From here follow narrow, cobbled High Street to reach the famous 18th century alehouse the **Olde Black Boy**, while around the corner in Scale Lane is the stylish, foody **Old House** with its focus on craft ale and high-end pub dining.

Continue into Silver Street to the **Olde White Hart** with its Theakston beers and a lineage stretching to the heart of the Civil War. From here cut down Trinity House Lane and Posterngate to arrive at Princes Dock where **Furley and Co** is a craft beer paradise.

If you can tear yourself away, cross the busy A63 to reach Humber Dock Street and walk alongside the bustling marina to visit **Humber Street Gallery**, where you can take in a little culture as well as beers from neighbours Yorkshire Brewing, before ending the crawl right on the waterfront at the **Minerva Hotel**, built in 1829 and an ideal place to relax and watch the business of life sliding by on the Humber.

In the city's main residential areas, north of the centre, are numerous other places worth visiting, like the **Station Inn** in Beverley Road and **Larkins** in Newland Avenue, named in honour of the city's poetic former son. In Princes Avenue, there are almost too many bars and restaurants to choose from, but you might want to try **Pave** where the drinker's choice stretches from the fiercely local to the eclectically continental

In run-down Wincolmlee is CAMRA favourite the **Whalebone** which celebrates, if that's the right word, the area's historic links to the Greenland whaling trade.

Yorkshire Dales Brewing Company

Yorkshire Dales Brewing Company Abbey Works, Askrigg, DL8 3JT;
T: 01969 622027;
E: rob@yorkshiredalesbrewery.com;
W: www.yorkshiredalesbrewery.com

Over the past 11 years, brewer Robert Wiltshire has created more than 540 different brews – cask, unfiltered craft keg and bottle conditioned – each with its own unique recipe. His success has seen the beers distributed widely across Yorkshire and an export deal to Germany, while a move into new premises has created a new American-influenced microbrewery experience. Several of the permanent beers reflect that influence, including the assertively citric American session ale **Butter Tubs** (3.7%), peachy **Nappa Scar** (4%) and **Askrigg Ale** (4.3%) an IPA whose big flush of tropical fruit is derived from Amarillo hops.

The Belgian helles-styled **Muker Silver** (4.1%), whose curious name honours a Swaledale village's silver band, demonstrates a continental leaning and exhibits more bitter, tart, fruity characteristics than you'd expect from a session-strength pint. Two more traditional British beers, the brown ale **Askrigg Bitter** (3.8%) and dark mild **Drover's Arms** (3.9%) complete the regular catalogue.

Yorkshire Heart Brewery

The Vineyard, Pool Lane,
Nun Monkton, York, YO26 8EL;
T: 01423 330716;
E: sales@yorkshireheart.com;
W: www.yorkshireheart.com

With a cider press being added to its vineyard and brewery, Yorkshire Heart has most of the major booze options covered; its new visitor centre will enhance its reputation as a top tourist attraction. As at Harthill Village Brewery, the name is ripe for beery puns, which include the smooth and coffee-ish mild **Darkheart** (4%), the full-bodied liquoricey stout **Blackheart** (4.8%) and the chestnut brown toffee-ish session ale **Hearty Bitter** (3.7%).

Vale of York Pubs

The Vale of York is a gentle plain rich in fertile farmland and sprinkled with wonderful pubs.

It's the heartland for one of the county's most up-market pub chains, Provenance Inns, whose hostelries each offer good beer and quality dining; several boast first-class overnight accommodation. The **Punch Bowl** at Marton cum Grafton, **Oak Tree** at Helperby, **Crown and Cushion** at Welburn and **Durham Inn** at Crayke have each been given the Provenance treatment, and all are thriving.

Close to Crayke, the **Bay Tree** at Stillington is another where the owners' attention to detail has created a rather beautiful country pub and restaurant.

You'll also find great food, much of it foraged or locally sourced at the **Alice Hawthorn** in Nun Monkton, something of a dead-end village a few miles north west of York. Further out, in the same direction is the 16th century **Crown Inn** at Roecliffe, with its sturdy stone structure, fine pub dining and four beautifully appointed bedrooms.

East of the city, **Suddaby's** in Malton and the **White Swan** in Thornton le Clay have both been recommended by breweries as the ideal place to sample their ales.

This handful offers just a flavour of the pleasures out there. Go explore.

Zapato Brewery

Slaithwaite, near Huddersfield.
E: info@zapatobrewery.co.uk;
W: www.zapatobrewery.co.uk

Beer consultant Matt Gorecki, a big noise behind Manchester's Indyman and Leeds's own Hop City festivals, cut his teeth with the North Bar group before establishing his own cuckoo brewery, using spare capacity at Northern Monk, Kirkstall and Atom – and named after Mexico's anarcho-leftist Zapatistas. "Our mission statement was that we would do nothing under 5% and use lots of oats in everything," he tells me over his cloudy pale and juicy **Hi-Pa** (5.2%) in the Turk's Head in Leeds. He describes export-style porter **Doom** (6%) as a "base beer" to which he can add salted  liquorice, coffee and nut flavourings depending on his mood. "And this from someone who thought you should never put flavourings in beer," he adds.

Matt cites Buxton, Northern Monk, Cloudwater and Magic Rock as the inspirational brewers against which he judges his own effort: "The current beer scene is ridiculously creative," he says. "Brewers like these have shown us that the possibilities are almost infinite – and people want it. What we're drinking now might have changed massively, but it's still good, it's still beer – and it's still about how it makes you feel."

CREATORS & PURVEYORS
OF MODERN PALE ALES*
IN CASK, KEG, CAN & BOTTLE.

YPA

24/7

Baby-Faced Assassin

Yankee

Buckeye

Highway 51

*AND OTHER STYLES OF BEER
WWW.ROOSTERS.CO.UK

ROOSTER^s
FREE RANGE BEERS FROM KNARESBOROUGH

Acknowledgments

Thanks are due to all those breweries who were kind enough to help me by submitting details for inclusion in the book. Also thanks to that tall and talented jam tart Gavin Aitchison, for many years the beer writer on the Yorkshire Evening Press, who was kind enough to help me put together the York pub crawl on p37-38; while my old friend Sue Underwood brought her local knowledge to bear on the Huddersfield pub crawl. Many of the other pub recommendations came from the brewers themselves. A number of people were selfless enough to pitch in with their tasting notes on several of these beers. They include Ben Jenkins, Gareth Dunworth, Rachel and Steve Brokenshar, Mike and Nicky Massen. Thanks also to Nick Love who contributed the article on the New Inn at Cropton (p75) and to David Burrill at Great Northern Books for his encouragement throughout the long horizonless watches of this book's creation.

Picture credits

The vast majority of images in this book were taken by the author. The pictures of The Maltings (p15) appear with the kind permission of the OnTrade Preview; Beak beers (p20-21) is by Chloe Grayson www.chloegrayson.com; Black Sheep Brewery (p26-27) by courtesy of the brewery; Pivni, York Tap and House of Trembling Madness (p37-38) by Ben Jenkins; Bricknell beers (p39) by Richard English; Bier Huis (p80) by David Jones; Blues Bar (p83) by Katherine Roberton-Warburton; The Mission (p127) by Katrina Jenkins; The Olde White Harte (p184) and Minerva (p185) are by Karen Esgate and Tapped Leeds (p163) by Tapped Brew Co. The Bingley Arms (p46-47), The New Inn (p75), Shibden Mill (p78-9), Three Pigeons (p79), Old Bell (p82), Nook (p119), Northern Monk (p124) and North Riding (p148-9) by courtesy of Yorkshire Post Newspapers. Pictures of the Cleveland Tontine (p133), Carpenters Arms (p132), Crown and Cushion (p187) and Durham Ox (p186) are by courtesy of Provenance Inns.

Pubs Index

Apart from some minor adjustments to assist the design, all the breweries in the book are listed alphabetically, while each of the pubs and pub crawls are scattered throughout, usually placed next to my description of an appropriate brewery, but here's a useful guide to help you find them: